Parenting Teens

A Parent's Guide for Children Who Are Growing Up and Moving on

(All You Need to Know About the First Two Years of Your Child's Life)

Jeffrey House

Published by Rob Miles

© Jeffrey House

All Rights Reserved

Parenting Teens: A Parent's Guide for Children Who Are Growing Up and Moving on (All You Need to Know About the First Two Years of Your Child's Life)

ISBN 9781990084416

All rights reserved. No part of this guide may be reproduced in any form without permission in writing from the publisher except in the case of brief quotations embodied in critical articles or reviews.

Legal & Disclaimer

The information contained in this book is not designed to replace or take the place of any form of medicine or professional medical advice. The information in this book has been provided for educational and entertainment purposes only.

The information contained in this book has been compiled from sources deemed reliable, and it is accurate to the best of the Author's knowledge; however, the Author cannot guarantee its accuracy and validity and cannot be held liable for any errors or omissions. Changes are periodically made to this book. You must consult your doctor or get professional medical advice before using any of the suggested remedies, techniques, or information in this book.

Upon using the information contained in this book, you agree to hold harmless the Author from and against any damages, costs, and expenses, including any legal fees potentially resulting from the application of any of the information provided by this guide. This disclaimer applies to any damages or injury caused by the use and application, whether directly or indirectly, of any advice or information presented, whether for breach of contract, tort, negligence, personal injury, criminal intent, or under any other cause of action.

You agree to accept all risks of using the information presented inside this book. You need to consult a professional medical practitioner in order to ensure you are both able and healthy enough to participate in this program.

Table of Contents

INTRODUCTION 1

CHAPTER 1: THE DIVORCE 3

CHAPTER 2: THREE CRITICAL PARENTING ROLES 9

CHAPTER 3: POSITIVE PARENTING AND EXPANDING YOUR CHILD'S SELF ESTEEM 28

CHAPTER 4: BE PROACTIVE INSTEAD OF BEING REACTIVE 31

CHAPTER 5: RESPONSES TO DIVORCE BY CHILDREN 35

CHAPTER 6: WHAT CAN PARENTS DO? 43

CHAPTER 7: HELP WITH STEP DAD PROBLEMS 47

CHAPTER 8: WHAT IS ADDICTION 56

CHAPTER 9: PRESENTING A UNIFIED FRONT 60

CHAPTER 10 67

CHAPTER 11: HOW DO YOU DISCIPLINE A TODDLER? 79

CHAPTER 12: CHILDHOOD WORRIES AND ANXIETY 85

CHAPTER 13: HOW CHILDREN SUCCEED 90

CHAPTER 14: TAKING CARE OF THE CHILDREN AFTER A DIVORCE 95

CHAPTER 15: WHAT YOU CAN DO TO ENSURE HEALTHY SCHOOL LUNCHES ARE AVAILABLE TO YOUR CHILDREN 102

CHAPTER 16: PARENTING STYLES AND DIANA BAUMRIND THEORY 106

CHAPTER 17: CRAFTING WITH KIDS 118

CHAPTER 18: TIPS FOR BUILDING HAPPINESS 124

CHAPTER 19: THE BOMB SITE BEDROOM 131

CHAPTER 20: HELPING YOUR CHILD EMBRACE INDIVIDUALITY 141

CHAPTER 21: MAKE TIME 146

CHAPTER 22: THE AFTER EFFECTS OF DIVORCE 150

CHAPTER 23: MAPPING YOUR CHILD'S ADVENTURE 160

CHAPTER 24: HOW TO KEEP EMOTIONALLY STRONG 168

CHAPTER 25: INEVITABLE LEADERSHIP SKILLS THAT YOU CAN INSTILL IN YOUR CHILD. 171

CHAPTER 26: EMOTIONS AND COMMUNICATION 179

CONCLUSION 187

Introduction

Single parenting is a growing epidemic throughout the world.As divorce is widely embraced and the concept of marriage is fizzling away, combined with the never ending high percentages of teenage pregnancy, single parenting is something that we are being forced to embrace.

What are the affects of single parenting on the children, kids and teenagers involved?Before people choose to become a single parent or sign the divorce papers, is there any research done about the perils of single parenting or the effects on the children?If there is, it must be minimal because who would want to put a child through so much emotional trauma.

Single parenting is extremely hard work for the parent involved, and often empathy is given to the single mother or father that is raising the kids.However, what about the children involved and what they are experiencing?There are undeniable statistics and facts about how single parenting affects the children and teens involved.The effects of single parenting are very broad and hit many areas including academics, emotional and behavioral disorders, anger issues, social issues and the list goes on.

Learning about what is involved in single parenting and what it does to our children is important.Being aware of why today's children may have emotional and physical deficits as a result of being raised by a single parent is important for understanding society today.Putting an end to single parenting may be an uphill battle that cannot be beat, but keeping parents together, and avoiding more teenage pregnancies is a challenge that can be undertaken.

People only get one childhood, there has to be a way not to rob them of that joy.

Chapter 1: The Divorce

When a couple split up, they don't just move apart when there are kids involved. Divorce is the end of the relationship and when a man is thrown into full time parenthood, it can be very difficult indeed. The baggage from the divorce is an emotional weight upon his shoulders. As he goes about his everyday tasks, he has a huge balancing act to perform. What many parents don't realize is how adaptable and resilient kids are but they do need a little coaxing. When the divorce happens and the children are placed with the father, they are in a space in their lives when the whole foundation of their home lives has been pulled away from under their feet. No matter whose fault it was, one parent is left to look after the children of the marriage and if it's the man, he has his work cut out for him.

I think that one of the kindest things that my father did was to tell us that both parents cared for the children and that the divorce was nothing to do with us. There was a certain reassurance in those words as children can often feel that they were to blame for the situation, no matter how far-fetched that seems to be. When words of anger are bandied about, children look at things differently to their parents. We saw things going wrong between our parents and every time they were aware of us hearing them arguing, they would close the door. For adults, this makes perfect sense. They don't want the children to hear all the anger. It's a way of protecting the children. However, from a child's point of view it locks them out of what's going on within the family unit and it leaves doubts as to whether they are being locked out because it's their fault.

It's important for a father to let his kids know that the divorce is something that was nothing to do with his relationship to the children. At this time, they may need extra reassurance, particularly if they are young children. They may be filled with all kinds of questions that you are not yet ready for, but in their minds, these are important questions. Be prepared because, at this stage, it really can make a difference to their lives and to your relationship with them how you answer their questions. Don't dismiss them by telling them not to worry. That shuts them out as well.

It's a good idea to have a sit down and talk with your kids. "Mommy and I are going to be living in different houses, but you're staying here with me," gives them reassurance in one way because they know where their lives are going and that's a great thing for a kid to know but of course they will question about seeing mommy. If there is anger and animosity between you, try to keep this to a minimum in front of the children. "Mommy has a new life, but she still loves you and wants to see you," is a wise answer.

What happens after the divorce is that jealousy and anger can get in the way of good parenting. You find yourself using the kids to spy on her and asking them all kinds of questions after a visitation. Try to avoid this if you can because it places the kids in a very vulnerable situation and shows lack of confidence as a father. Your kids need strength right now, rather than getting involved in arguments between their parents. You will feel less guilt if you don't use your kids as go-betweens. Think of your life with them as a complete thing. You have control of the children. Your rules are the rules they must now live by but in a very positive way.

My father was an extremely positive person who shared loads of experiences with us and that's what you need to work on right now. You may not be good at cooking and doing all the chores that are involved in looking after children but if you level with them and stop making excuses, they are very likely to understand your situation and help you to become a good father. For example, it doesn't hurt to tell them you are struggling but that you will get through this together and to enlist their help. It makes them feel loved and needed and is a great way for a father to forge a strong relationship with his kids.

Why are you feeling so guilty?

The chances are, if you have been through a messy divorce, you feel like you haven't given the kids the support that they need and the guilt that this brings can be enormous. You may not have the same organizational ability as your ex-wife, but letting the kids know this rather than keeping that guilt inside can help them to help you. "Daddy doesn't know how to fold this," may be greeted with a child being only too happy to show daddy. After all, the child has seen the job done and can help out and will gladly do so if daddy drops all the defensive stance and lets the child into his life in that capacity.

I remember my father struggling with ironing and I must have only been about eight at the time, but teaching him was a real pleasure and helped us to bond as people. If you don't know how to do things, don't feel guilty about it. Enlist the help of the kids because they have some amazing lessons to give to you. A parent child relationship is a two-way thing and there's no need for a parent to feel guilty about not always being the strong part of the relationship. Admit your faults. Kids will help you and they will have their fair share of weaknesses too that you need to accept as being part of who they are.

Chapter 2: Three Critical Parenting Roles

Now we're going to talk about three over-arching roles that are intertwined – i.e., in any situation your primary role may be as a caregiver, but you are also learning by observing so you can then take advantage of teaching moments that arise. Keeping in mind that the core foundations are Caring and Consistency, three essential parenting roles are:

CULTIVATOR – promoting, developing and nurturing

CHALLENGER – teaching, questioning, and reinforcing

CHEERLEADER – praising, valuing, and supporting

CULTIVATOR

To Cultivate means to nurture and develop, as in gardening or farming or growing a business. A gardener must have a certain level of knowledge and skill in order to be successful in growing fruit or flowers. Gardeners become highly skilled in reading the weather, observing the health of their plants, and mitigating potential damage that might be caused by poor soil or dry weather. They decide when to plant, when to fertilize and with what products, and when to spray for insects. If they miss certain windows of opportunity, their crops will not grow as well – or at all.

So it is with parenting. There's a lot of care-giving involved, especially in the younger years. This isn't always the most fun part, and can be hard sometimes; but even in infancy positive nurturing and care-giving is essential. Nurturing your children means positive touching and loving talk, even when changing dirty diapers or cleaning up food off the floor. Most of us don't think about all the developmental stages because babies are so cute, but taking loving care of them through their colic and dribbles and throwing food stages is critical to their positive development later on.

Cultivating is also about discipline – planting in rows rather than willy-nilly, pulling the weeds, pruning the plants, applying fertilizer, and watering regularly. For some kids, a "look" (or even a lecture) will suffice to stop certain behaviors, while others require more concrete penalties – a time-out in their room (no more than 5 to 15 minutes usually makes the point), or with-holding television or phone privileges. Whatever you do will likely result in some conversations about what's fair, and what's not fair – does the punishment fit the crime? Answers are very elusive, since all kids and families are different – but 5 minutes to a 2-year-old can seem like an eternity, so be sure to use age-appropriate consequences.

A word about neglect and abuse.

Neglect can be as simple as often ignoring your baby when they cry because they're hungry or their diaper is wet, which turns into abuse when this happens every day. Or leaving them to swelter in a too-hot car, or not changing their diaper when needed. When farmers neglect their fields – no plowing, no fertilizer, no spraying – the fields become choked with weeds; and if neglected long enough, become virtually un-usable.

When parents neglect their children – no hugs, no conversations, no happy times – the children become frustrated, negative, and withdrawn. This has been demonstrated time and again by studying children in orphanages – even with sufficient food and shelter, when there's little touching or conversation or positive feedback, the children become very quiet and inhibited, lose weight, and are often way behind in physical coordination, speech development, and intellectual development. These deficiencies remain throughout their lives.

If this neglect is paired with abuse, or negative interactions such as hitting, yelling, or shaking, then children become actively hostile toward others. Spanking, even with your hand, is also abuse — spanking is hitting, and is done in anger, not love. We know that when abuse continues over time, children act out in school, and often skip school; thereby losing more ground academically and socially, and may ultimately end up on the wrong end of the law.

We would wonder about the sanity of a gardener that planted a garden, failed to weed and water the plants, and then started hitting and tearing them up because they didn't grow. But we see this happening with children!

So, in the role of CULTIVATOR, parenting skills include:

Assure proper food and shelter — nutritious food, a safe place to eat and sleep, clothing appropriate for the weather. When children are routinely given pizza and fast foods, we know that they can become addicted to salt, fat and sugar; often resulting in obesity and future health problems.

Loving physical interactions – hugs, kisses, pats on the head – all conveying that the 'self' is valuable, and valued; critical for positive emotional and social development.

Conversations about their world – a book, pictures, birds in the trees – even (maybe especially) with infants. We know that infants learn language from Day 1 – they hear the cadence of their primary language from children and adults around them, and begin babbling and sounding out words within weeks.

Name and count things, repeating colors and shapes – all build the architecture of your child's mind. In the grocery store, name fruits and vegetables, count them out, name their colors over and over.

Take a walk and put names to common objects – trees, cars, animals – along with colors and shapes. This teaches vocabulary words, and attaches meaning to objects all around us.

Exposure to art and music – there's more research today about the important role that art and music play in cognitive development. Our brains react to auditory sounds – music and voices – from infancy; developing synapses or connections. Same with art – color, form, movement – that also expands our minds and forms complex neural networks.

Loving words, softly spoken – for comfort, safety, love. Little research is available on the impact of war on children; but we know that children exposed to routine gunfire and sounds of war, and to death – especially of family members – are often angry and hostile, growing up to become more cannon fodder.

CHALLENGER

Another role of parenting that is often overlooked is what I call the role of Challenger. In this role, parents also need to know their kids – what they like and how they learn. This takes lots of time – knowing another person, even your own children, is not easy; and is sometimes ever-changing.

Every child is different than any other from the time they're laid in your arms, born with certain pre-dispositions that we still don't fully understand. In your role as a parent, you learn about each child by watching them, touching them, and talking to them. When they cry, what they are afraid of in the night or on the playground, who they seem to like or not like – all of this information is very important when helping them grow in a positive way.

So, there's David, who's quiet and doesn't talk much; but seems to watch everyone and everything. Jill talks and runs around a lot, paying most attention to her own activities and toys. And Jason just seems to want to climb trees and play in the woods.

So, as a Challenger, your role is to help each of them develop well-rounded skills that you know are important in everyday life. All of us have to get along with other people, for example; so David must learn how to talk to others enough to make his needs known, as well as to get along in a group – a skill many adults don't seem to have learned yet!

Jill is social and talkative, so she may have to learn how to listen more to other people – so you might challenge her by simply insisting she keep quiet while David is encouraged to have his say as well, albeit more slowly.

Jill begins developing patience, and David learns that he is also valued by being encouraged to speak up. Then there's Jason – he may have to be challenged to sit at the dinner table until everyone is finished. These are very small steps that must be taken consistently on a daily basis so that certain habits are formed.

Developing habits requires consistent work, and is very hard for all of us. We have to challenge ourselves to be more patient, less or more talkative, or to sit still during those college lectures. Letting your children know that you, too, are working on certain skills lets them know that they're still OK because we're all learning. In this way, you validate (i.e., cultivate) their value to you and to others.

So in the role of Challenger, some parenting skills include:

Teach basic rules of conduct, such as sitting at the dinner table – for toddlers, it may be 5 minutes; and you 'up the ante' for your 5-year-old, 7-year-old and 10-year-old. Sounds basic, but it's amazing how many parents simply give up trying – and routinely f56acquiesce to pizza on the run.

Practice learning a new skill – jump-rope, skipping rocks on a lake, riding a bicycle. OK, so this happens all the time – or does it? Playing with your kids once a month isn't the same as helping them on a regular basis with consistent drill and practice.

Challenge them to repeat a list of fruits or vegetables they know, or name everything that's green, or count from 1 to 10, then 1 to 20, and so on. Little steps, big learnings.

Ask questions about their homework. First of all, they need to develop the responsibility of doing their homework – consistent practice – and then using those skills in other ways. And they need to know that homework is important – to you, and to others – to develop focus, concentration, and problem-solving skills.

Have them explain to you why adding and subtracting is important – or better yet, have them count change with you at the grocery store. If learning is important, why is it important – making the connection to 'real life' is essential to motivate kids and adults.

Assign chores to all your children, based on their skill level, beginning about age 4-5 years – some parents begin even earlier. Every child wants to be an adult like Mommy and Daddy – so let them know that these are things that adults do, and need to do well.

All of us have chores to do that we don't like — but kids should make their own beds, pick up after themselves, fix their own lunches, help younger siblings learn to hold silverware, etc. This teaches the responsibilities that come with belonging to any group — a family, a church, a sports team.

Sit with your kids as they read books or play Monopoly, and challenge them to read bigger words, or words they've never seen before. This creates emotional bonds, as well as teaching relevant skills.

While driving, have them help you watch for the exit signs you need to get home, or read the street signs on the way. GPS is a wonderful thing, but as available as it is, learning to read in practical situations is far more important.

CHEERLEADER

We don't think of ourselves as cheerleaders, but think about what cheerleaders do. They praise their team and team members, they inspire, they get people excited about what they're doing, and motivate them to come back for more.

And they do this consistently, even when there's no game – or when the team is losing. It doesn't mean that they're always 'on,' but that others are inspired by them in all types of situations. So it is with parenting. If you are positive and excited about what's happening, your kids will be positive and excited about it as well.

Children learn what they live. If they live in a positive home where parents are enthusiastic about learning and applying information, then they will also be excited about learning and going to school. Praising your children for positive behaviors, for learning new skills, and for being dressed up for a special occasion, means that they learn to value themselves and others, developing positive self-esteem.

Self-esteem is critical for all of us, since it gives us enough confidence to try new things and not be put-off by failure, which we all experience. Learning cannot take place without sufficient self-esteem and confidence, and knowing how to build on previous skills.

On the other hand, when you don't care about your school or your community, but continually make negative comments about teachers or your neighbors or the church minister, then your kids will also learn to not care – and they are much more likely to misbehave in the grocery store, at church and in school.

When we are negative or indifferent, then our children also become negative and indifferent. Your children will model your behavior and your words, and sometimes this can happen in a most embarrassing place!

Cheerleaders cheer even when a team is losing. It's important to praise your children for trying – and trying again to overcome failure. Cheering our kids on is essential for learning and growing. If we are laughed at or punished when we try something and fail, we're not likely to try it again.

At the same time, observe what Jason did wrong, or couldn't do well in order to finish the task – and then challenge him to try it again, maybe in a different way. Enlist David's help – this creates (and also reinforces) a team effort, enhances David's skill level, and helps Jason know that he can learn from his peers, not just adults. These are all very important skills and understandings for kids to develop.

Being a cheerleader also means modeling the behaviors you want in your children. We all yell at our kids and our spouses, but sincerely apologizing for it means that your kids learn two things – we all make mistakes, but there are ways to lessen the damage that's done.

They learn about relationships, how to build them and keep them…..something that not all adults know how to do! These skills are all part of learning how to get along in groups of all types — as you ask questions, your kids learn that it's OK to ask; as you do your chores, kids learn that everyone needs to pitch in for success; and as you try new things (food, games, woodworking, etc.), your kids learn to try new things as well.

So some specific things you can do as a CHEERLEADER include:

Teach them new words, showing them how to use a dictionary (online or in the library), and praising them when they find a word to teach you!

Praise efforts at trying and failing, as well as successful completion of chores, and learning new skills.

Consistently inspect and value their completed work.

Try new things with your kids, whether it's learning how to play a new computer game, or riding safely on an ATV, or a new woodworking project.

Inspire your kids by being excited about your own world — watching a documentary on ocean life, or becoming active in a political campaign, or simply volunteering at school or the local food bank.

Encourage them to talk about their day – and when a teacher sends a positive note home, let Jill tell you all about it, and praise her for work well done or for good conduct.

Show that you value learning by making sure Jason does his homework, and does it well; and by paying attention to getting a 'B-plus' instead of the 'C-minus' he got last week.

Use incentives where appropriate to encourage learning and good behavior. This can be a tough one, but we all do better if we get some chocolate when we've done the dishes.

Model good, positive behaviors – if you want your kids to read, they must see you reading, or it's clear that it's not of value to you, and therefore not to them either. If you leave your chores undone, they'll leave their chores undone, no matter how much you yell or plead with them. They will copy your table manners, and the way you talk to them and others.

Model positive attitudes. If you tear down their school and their teachers, they will act out in school, and refuse to learn. If you gossip about the grocery store manager, your pastor and your neighbors, they will spread the stories, and embellish them with stories of their own.

Inspire them to show respect and trust in themselves and in other people by modeling respect and trust. Praise them when they help an older person across the street, or stop the car at a crosswalk.

Teach them who they can trust, and how to treat strangers with respect and caution.

Basic stuff, right? But often hard to put into practice. None of this is rocket science – mostly just plain good common sense. But just as Rome wasn't built in a day, so children aren't raised in a day with just one or two simple demonstrations during their life. It takes planning, doing, evaluating and planning again.

A journey begins with one step, one foot consistently put in front of the other. A journey continues when we are positively encouraged, challenged and inspired to do more than we've done before – otherwise there's no journey. We begin learning at birth, and the first five years of life establish the foundation for the rest of our lives – positive or negative.

Play is a child's work for not only developing physical skills, but also language, cognitive flexibility and problem-solving skills, positive relationships and job success. Learning and achieving can, and should, be challenging and fun for all of us.

So, **Care** enough to **Consistently Cultivate, Challenge and Inspire** your children; and they will reward you with a positive, caring, and SMART adult.

Chapter 3: Positive Parenting And Expanding Your Child's Self Esteem

Are you looking for a great way to expand your child's self esteem? You can start by using positive parenting which means showing them your positive sense of self and how strong your self esteem is. Showing confidence anytime you speak helps to demonstrate all of your strengths. Our kids learn from their environment and the people around them. They learn from their daily routine and all the activities they are exposed to.

Giving your kids honest and positive praise will reap great rewards. Look everyday for that something that you can praise them for. Use their daily tasks or chores around the house that you want them to do and praise them for a job well done when they complete them. Show them that their positive actions are worthy of positive praise.

We need to communicate openly whenever our kids seem depressed, sad or angry. Show them complete honesty and be patient with them. It can be hard for them to understand what they are feeling let alone why. Being a good listener without being judgmental will make them feel comfortable to open up to you so that you can help them sort out what is going on. Be sure to leave the back door open for them by suggesting positive behaviors as resolutions. This lets them know that the next time they are not feeling good they know they can come to you for help without any consequences or repercussions.

It is important to teach our kids how important it is to set some goals and develop plans to accomplish those goals by completing all the defined tasks. Have them start with small projects. Review their goals to make sure the activities to complete them are appropriate and not too complicated for them. Monitor their progress so you can praise them during the project as well as at the end.

One of the most important things you can do everyday to expand your child's self esteem is to tell them I love you. Even if their behavior is less then positive you need to remind yourself that it's not them you don't like, just their behavior. Send them a job well done card in the mail or put a note in their pocket or lunch bag. You will be surprised how quickly then can say I love you back.

Chapter 4: Be Proactive Instead Of Being Reactive

Most of the parents' failure in parenting resulted from being more reactive to their children's behaviors and actions. It is so easy to get caught up in the moment. The adolescents usually look into the behavior of their parents for them and on the things that they do.If their parents continually react on the things that they do, teenagers often shrink down from them.

Teenagers are very keen observers especially to the facial expressions of their parents, their gestures, and most importantly to the way we speak to them.Once they observe some undercurrent in which they perceive to be more likely negative in nature, meaning, against them, they often have ready retaliations to it.The following could help parents be more pro-active towards their children rather than being re-active.

It is very important that we give the child ample time to explain before opening up our mouth to nag or give lecture and obviously reacting to what they say.Through giving enough time, every angle can also be well viewed and possibilities for a better answer could be better determined.By giving them more time to speak up, parents would readily know the root of their behavior, their inner turmoil, as well as their wants.On the other hand, parents too could compose themselves and give more controlled reactions. It is almost like the old saying of "count to ten". I know it is hard sometimes the child lies to get out of trouble and we as parents must decipher all of this explanation and the lies makes us angry. I understand that!! It is normal believe me, but we ARE the adults here and we ARE the role models to our child's life. So we as parents need to keep our composer, and listening skills, believe me once you start doing this, letting the child speak more, the child WILL open up more and more and most likely than not the lies will decrease and the trust increases. What you got to lose, sounds like a win-win.

In giving feedbacks, always bear in mind to check the words used, the gestures, as well as the facial expression.Parents who get angrier than their child does never show confidence; instead, it only shows that they could never handle the situation well too.As much as possible, parents should be more passive but in such a way that they could also give good impact to their children.

Bear in mind also that children have feelings, which could be hurt.Thus, hurting their feelings can be avoided by remembering that they should be respected.Initially, parents too hurt themselves more if they see themselves hurting their child by what they say or do.Thus, as much as possible, parents should try to hold on to their temper.Once the child sees that, the parent's are losing their temper and their composure. Then for sure, they would always feel that it could always be alright to do the same.

In times of confrontation with the children, it is always wise that parents should listen first, to what their children need to say.By being pro-active, parents should let their children rant until such time that they have nothing more to say.By so doing, parents are able to get through the roots of their children's anger and at the same time, children could say all the things that they want to say to them and will have more time to listen to what their parents need to say later on.

By being pro-active too, parents are becoming models to their children.If their children could see that their parents are becoming more of being proactive rather than being reactive, they too could have a chance in changing their ways and be more like their parents.Whatever the children do reflect how their parents have brought them up, and this is what parents should always remember in dealing with them.

Chapter 5: Responses To Divorce By Children

All children, no matter what their age or developmental stage will experience some effects of the divorce. In the case of very young infants they may not express these issues verbally; however you may notice a change in behavior during the divorce and then may see other issues later as the child matures. Older kids may indicate they accept the divorce, but there may feel torn or hurt about the breakup of the family.

UNDERSTANDING THE GRIEF CYCLE

Typically children will go through a grief cycle when parents divorce. Each child, depending on their age, their personality and their ongoing contact or lack of contact with both parents will experience divorce in slightly different ways.

Most kids will experience the following phases during the divorce and the time period of about a year immediately after the divorce. Each child will be slightly different their expression of these phases or stages, but typical reactions will include both emotional and behavioral changes that can be worrisome and even problematic for parents.

DENIAL

Kids in denial simply don't want to accept the fact that Mom and Dad are getting a divorce. During the denial stage, and all through the divorce, parents have to be very positive about the other parent and must keep any explanations about the divorce or separation simple and to the basic issues as they relate to the kids. Important questions to answer include:

- ☐ Where the child is going to live
- ☐ When the child will get to see both parents

- ☐ Ongoing expressions of love from both parents towards the child
- ☐ Good, positive and respectful comments about the other parent
- ☐ Simple, concise explanations about divorce that are age appropriate and not negative about the other parents character or behavior

Most kids will be in the denial stage for 6-8 weeks, sometimes longer if there has been a previous separation. If humanly possible set a schedule of parenting time immediately so the child doesn't feel rejected or abandoned by either parent.

ANGER

Kids will be angry going through the divorce for several reasons. These can include:

- ☐ Anger at themselves that they may have done something to cause the divorce
- ☐ Anger at a parent for leaving the home
- ☐ Anger at a parent for making the other parent leave
- ☐ Anger at the changes in their life

- ☐ Anger at being moved from Mom's to Dad's house and back again with no regard for their schedule, desires or wants
- ☐ Anger at lack of control in their lives
- ☐ Anger at the feelings of rejection and abandonment they may feel

ANXIETY

Kids often show anxiety in their behaviors more that they express it in words. Children showing anxiety may be more likely to:

- ☐ Have emotional outbursts at family members or at school
- ☐ Have eating, sleeping or behavioral disorders
- ☐ Complain of headaches, stomachaches and fatigue
- ☐ Need to have constant reassurance
- ☐ Want to be close to a parent all the time
- ☐ Insist on sleeping in the same bed or room as the parent

- ☐ Experience nightmares, anxiety attacks and withdraw from activities

CONFUSION

It is very normal for children to be confused about what is happening through the divorce. Whenever possible provide lots of structure, predictability and routine between Mom's house and Dad's house to eliminate or minimize confusion. Calendars, agendas, text messages, email reminders are all good ways to help keep children informed of the information they need to know regarding time with Mom, time with Dad, who is picking them up or where they are to go after school or on the weekend.

Be prepared to answer a lot of questions when kids are in this stage and do not become frustrated if you seem to be answering the same question over and over. If you find this is the case, try developing a way to help the child remember, turn it into a game or post messages on a board in the house to help keep things organized.

BARGAINING

Most children will go through a phase where they may attempt to bargain with Mom and Dad, or even a higher power, to attempt to bring the family back together. They may also bargain between brothers and sisters or between other family members to attempt a family reunification. It is important to keep kids focused on being kids and to keep reinforcing that they did not cause the divorce, nor can they "fix" the problem and reunite Mom and Dad.

DEPRESSION

Depression with children is common through divorce. They may seem to lose their sense of spontaneous joy, their ability to see the good in things, or their love of a particular hobby, pastime or activity. Encouraging our kids to stay involved and active and modeling being positive and future focused is the best option. Both parents need to let kids know that things are going to be different, but that they will still be loved, cared for and cherished, even though Mom and Dad are living in different homes.

If you are concerned about your child's emotional or mental state, seek a counselor or consult with your physician. Often speaking to someone outside the family that can help normalize the divorce for the child can help in overcoming any sadness or depression the child may be experiencing.

ACCEPTANCE

Once children accept the fact that the divorce is happening or has happened, and see that Mom and Dad are still Mom and Dad, still active in their lives and in their loving, supporting families most children will adjust to the divorce situation. Most children will take about a year to reach acceptance with Mom and Dad are co-parenting and communicating. The more conflict, negativity or neglect children experience from one or both parents the longer it will take them to accept the divorce and be able to look forward to their relationship with both parents.

Chapter 6: What Can Parents Do?

So what can parents do to raise their kids properly? The answer is very simple. Give them enough time. Sounds easy right? But it's actually one of the hardest things to do in a family. There's only 24 hours a day, 7 days a week, 30 days a month and all of these is not enough. People think that you have too much time in your hands, but in reality, you only have a couple of hours left with your kids. The best thing to do is make the most of it.

It doesn't matter if you're a full time mom or working dad, or if it's the other way around. It is very important that you set aside some time for your kids. It can be a couple of hours a day, enough to give you time to catch up with school, watch their favorite TV show or just spend some quality time together.

It's important that you create a schedule, one for your work and one for your family. As much as possible, keep your work and family separate from each other. When you go home, leave your problems at the office or temporarily forget it once you sit at the dinner table with your kids. Kids are very sensitive to their surroundings and they can sense if you're having a bad day. It will make them feel uncomfortable to talk to you during dinner and will most likely eat quietly, wanting to get out of the room as soon as possible.

Make your family time about your family and not about your work. True, you may have some rough times and problems to think about but your kid has one too. When you're a parent you'll realize that there are sacrifices you have to make and this is one of them. Being selfless and putting your kids first before yourself.

Aside from a schedule or timetable, you should also learn to set goals. Be it helping your kid do his math homework or attending your daughter's dance recital or watching football with your kids. Set small goals that have to do with spending time with you kids. Make a list of activities you'd like to do with them, places you want to visit. Then, ask your kids to do the same. Once you have your goals planned out, it is easier to squeeze in to the schedule that you're making.

When planning things, avoid making promises, especially if you're not sure you can fulfill it. It will only break your kid's heart and that's something you should try to avoid. At most, tell your kid that you will try to do your best. This way, even though your kids have expectations, they won't hold on to it as much as promises. But make sure that you really try your best to be able to do the stuffs you planned with them.

It's also important to hear what your kids have to say. Often time, parents think they are the only ones who can voice out opinions or give criticisms. This one sided communication backfires. Your kid will only learn to talk behind your back and harbor hard feelings. Once in a while, sit with your kids and ask them to rate your parenting skills or talk about their feelings towards you. Don't speak, don't make it about yourself and no matter how negative their words are, just listen. A good parent always knows how to listen. After that, thank your kids, give them a hug and reflect on what they said. Apologize and try to improve yourself.

Do the same thing for your kids. Have a heart to heart talk and this time explain to them why you feel the need to discipline them. Take this opportunity to help them understand you. This is your chance to set things straight and be on the same page.

Chapter 7: Help With Step Dad Problems

Men who marry women with children come to their new responsibilities with a mixed bag of emotions. Your motivations may be far different from those that make a man assume responsibility for his biological children.

As a new husband, you might react to your "instant" family with feelings that range from admiration to fright to contempt. You might even see yourself as less effective than a biological father. A new stepfather typically enters a household headed by a mother.

When a mother and her children make up a single-parent family, she tends to learn autonomy and self-confidence, and her children do more work around the house and take more responsibility in family decisions than do children in two-parent households.

These are good things, but to enter such a family, you must work your way into a closed group. For one thing, mom and kids share a common history, one that does not yet include you.

Moving into your wife's house can make you feel like the "odd man out." It might be months before you feel comfortable and at home. In truth, initially, stepfathers do have less power relative to stepchildren, particular adolescents, when they move into the mother-child home.

You might feel out of place because of a different background or because you have a different perspective on what family life is all about. After years of living as a single-parent family, for instance, both mom and kids are likely to have evolved a chore allocation system.

As a newcomer, especially if you assume the traditional male role in a two-earner remarriage, you may draw complaints that you are not contributing enough. Or, while you think it helpful not to interfere, your behavior might be seen as an unwillingness to contribute.

The "hidden agenda" is one of the first difficulties a stepfather runs into: The mother, her children, or both, may have expectations about what you will do, but may not give you a clear picture of what those expectations are. You may have a hidden agenda of your own.

You may see your new stepchildren as spoiled and unruly and decide they need discipline. Or, you may find that after years of privacy, a bustling house full of children disrupts your routine.

A part of the step-children's hidden agenda is the extent to which they will let you play the father. Children can be adamant in their distaste for, or jealousy of, their stepfather, or they may be ready and anxious to accept you as a "new daddy."

Stepfathers tend to be more distant and detached than stepmothers, and this is not necessarily a bad thing. Some detachment might be just what's needed in order to have a workable relationship with your stepchildren, especially during the early years of your marriage. Teenagers may be mature enough to think of you primarily as their mother's husband rather than as a stepfather.

Teens, and younger children, may be unwilling to go back to being "children"- that is, dependent on and subject to adult direction. To you, they may seem spoiled and undisciplined rather than mature.

Try to keep in mind that as part of a single-parent family, their responsibilities and participation in decisions were probably encouraged. The hidden agendas of mom, children, and you may be over simple matters of everyday living, things like food preferences, personal space, and the division of labor.

Discipline is likely to be particularly tricky for everyone. Two parents rather than one now establish house rules and influence the children's behavior, but you and your spouse may not agree. A second problem can be the influence of the biological father.

To you, there may sometimes seem to be three parents instead of two-especially if the non-custodial father sees the children regularly-with the biological father wielding more influence than you, the stepfather. The key is for everyone to work together.

You might react to all of this in one of four ways. First, you might be driven away. Second, you might take control, establishing yourself as undisputed head of the household, and force the former single-parent family to accommodate your preferences.

Third, you might assimilate into a family headed by a mother and have relatively little influence on the way things are done. And fourth, you, your new wife, your stepchildren, and their non-custodial biological father can all negotiate new ways of doing things by taking to heart and incorporating the information you are about to learn-the most positive alternative for everyone.

Okay. Now you have a pretty good feel for what everyone is going through. How do you start to make it better? How can you give yourself breathing space-time to catch your breath while your new family begins to come together emotionally and learns how to work together, a process that can take years?

First you must be very clear about what you want and expect from this marriage and the individuals involved, including yourself. What are you willing to do? What do you need from your spouse in order to feel supported physically and emotionally?

In a loving and positive way, now is the time to articulate, negotiate, and come to an agreement on your expectations and about how you and your partner will behave.

The best marriages are flexible marriages. But how can you be flexible if you do not know where you, your spouse, and the children stand and what everyone needs right now? Needs will change over time. There must be room for change.

People change and promises will not prevent change. People who vow never to change often try to hide their personal growth from each other, and the result, of course, is lost intimacy. People who are not flexible, who cannot change, may be left with a permanent, but stale, relationship.

In flexible marriages, partners are freer to reveal their changing selves and the parts of themselves that no longer fit into their old established patterns. You and your partner must continue to be in touch at a deep emotional level even when the outer framework of your lives changes.

The more you know, the more you grow. You couldn't possibly have known at the beginning of your new family what you know now and will learn later. Flexibility in your relationships will enable growth rather than tearing them apart.

Get in touch with your expectations and encourage every family member to do the same so you can compare and negotiate the differences. Your goal, and your partner's, are to actively begin to define and built a healthy, supportive relationship.

Talk over specific problems. Just because you were unable to predict some of the problems, don't let that stand in the way of dealing with them now.

It is not uncommon for people who marry again to feel reluctant to fully commit themselves emotionally, even though they want the marriage to work. The struggles of your first marriage and divorce can leave scars.

When not openly acknowledged and healed, past failure, rejection, loss, and guilt can undermine a new intimate relationship without either of you understanding what is happening.

One way to release these feelings is to share them, and to make it safe for your partner to do the same. Each of you needs to feel secure, respected, positive about yourself, and as comfortable as possible in your new family unit.

You may feel the "conflict taboo" even more than in your first marriage. It is understandable that you want to make this marriage work. You might feel too "battle-scarred" to open "a can of worms." And so, you gloss over differences that need airing and resolution-differences over which you may not have hesitated to wage war in your first marriage.

Avoiding airing your differences is a serious mistake. It is important for you to understand your own and your partner's needs because society hasn't a clue how step-families should work. Unless you talk about your expectations, they are likely to be unrealistic.

Chapter 8: What Is Addiction

Another issue that your teen could be dealing with is addiction. There are many things that your teen could be addicted to including drugs, alcohol, and internet porn to name a few. They may exhibit some behaviors that mimic normal teenager behaviors to the outside viewer, but there are things that you will be able to notice when you start to watch your teen act out more than before.

Addiction is a hard thing for your teenager to get through. Their brains are in the process of developing, and when you invite something like drugs or alcohol into the mix, it is going to really mess with this whole development and makes it harder than ever to get over the addiction. In fact, many teens have a harder time getting over addiction compared to adults who could be going through the same issues as well.

If you are worried that your child is going through an addiction and you want to recognize the signs to help them to get through this process and get them the assistance they need, you need to recognize the signs of addiction. Some of the most common signs of addiction include:

Changes in Physical Appearance

The first thing that you should check for in your teenager is their physical appearance. Take a look into their eyes. Do you notice that the eyes are bloodshot or that the pupils are dilated? These can be signs of drug use or even using stimulants. You should also check out how their health is doing. If there are changes in their hygiene, sleeping habits, weight, and appetite, there is often an issue with substance abuse, but since these can show other health issues as well, you should get your child evaluated before jumping to conclusions about drug use.

Trouble With School

This is especially important to note if your child did really well in school before and now they are having trouble. You will notice that their grades are taking a nosedive, even in classes that they used to love, and they are getting into more trouble than before and skipping out on some of their classes rather than attending.

Changes in Activities

For the most part, your child will have activities that they love to do. These are the activities that they did after school or with some friends. If all of a sudden your child shows no interest in these activities and is not replacing them with something new or doing anything at all, there could be an issue. You will also need to look out for changes in their friends. If they have stopped hanging out with one group of friends in favor of another, this group could be getting them into some trouble.

Changes in Behavior

You will need to pay attention to how your child is acting at home, and if possible, see if you can get an opinion on how your child is behaving when they are out of home as well. If you start to notice that they are acting depressed and angry, there is a big change in their appearance, mood swings that change often, asking for a lot more privacy, and being isolated from others, you should seek some help.

Figuring out whether your teenager is dealing with an addiction is never easy. There are a lot of things that need to come into play and often the behaviors could be mixed up with normal behavior or even depression. If you are unsure about whether your child has an addiction or not, bring in another opinion and get your child the help that they need as soon as possible.

Chapter 9: Presenting A Unified Front

One of the main reasons that children misbehave is because their parents are not in agreement with the type of discipline that should be used. This often leads to children not being disciplined at all. When parents cannot present a unified front to their children it is very dangerous and can lead to rebellion down the road. However, there are things that you can do in order to present a unified front to your children.

Together, discuss the rules that should be followed in your home as well as the types of discipline that will be used. Make sure that the two of you agree on the discipline as well as the rules in the home.

Never argue in front of your children or where they can hear you – this is especially important if the disagreement is over discipline or the children's behavior. If you have a disagreement with the other parent, make sure to discuss it when the child is asleep and discuss it quietly. Make sure that neither of you are angry and that you have had time to think about the situation.

Never contradict each other in front of the child. If a child thinks that there are sides to take, that both of you do not agree to the rules, he will take the side that he thinks will benefit him the most. This is how children divide and conquer, and you cannot allow them to do so. Remember to wait until the two of you are alone to discuss the issue, then make sure you both agree on the rules so next time there are no questions.

Make sure that the parent that administers the discipline is the one to speak to the child afterwards. You do not want one parent disciplining while the other parent cuddles the child. Let the parent that carried out the discipline be the one to talk to the child afterwards, so as to show him that discipline is a form of love.

Make sure that your words match your actions. This is just one more way that you can put up a unified front. If our words do not match our actions, it means that we are not unified, and our children will pick up on this quickly. You want to make sure that your children do not look at you as a hypocrite. For example, if you do not want your children to smoke when they are older, it is important that you do not smoke either.

You need to ensure that your children always know that you will back up the other parent. One way to do this is to make the consequence stricter if, in an attempt to get a lighter sentence, a child tries to appeal to the parent that did not administer the discipline. Children will learn quickly that both of the parents are on the same side and they cannot be divided.

You should make sure that the kids know the rules as well as the consequences in advance. Don't make a rule after the child has done something wrong – springing a new rule on him will make him think that you are not being fair. If you do this, it will cause the child to rebel in the future, and you cannot present a unified front of you do not know the rules ahead of time.

Make sure that all of the authority is unified. You want to make sure that grandma knows the rules, that the sitter knows the rules, that you back up the teachers and the coaches as well. This will ensure that the child knows he has to follow the rules. Of course, there are a few exceptions to backing up others in authority, but those are personal beliefs and choices that you will have to make on your own.

One thing that you have to remember is that if you feel that a teacher or other figure of authority has disciplined your child wrongfully, you need to speak to them in private so the child does not hear what you are saying. This will ensure that the child believes you are still unified and agree with the discipline.

You do need to remember that not all authority is equal when it comes to your child. You are the top authority and no one can go above you, be it the baby sitter, the grandparents, or even a school teacher. You have the final say in how your child is disciplined.

As we learn how to discipline our children and choose what techniques we will use, we have to remember that we as parents might not have been disciplined in the same manner when we were growing up. Both parents, having grown up in different homes, were raised by different people with different discipline styles. Of course each parent is going to think that the way they were raised is the best way, but at some point the two of you have to sit down and create your own way of disciplining, either by combining the great points from the way both of you were raised or by creating an entirely new method.

Agree to disagree on some issues. There are going to be some topics on which you simply cannot agree. For example, some parents think that their children should be given an allowance while others do not. If your partner thinks that your child should have an allowance and you do not, allow your partner to take care of the allowance. Make sure the child understands that you are not part of his getting allowance and there will be no advances made by you if he gets short on cash. Of course, this is an issue you will face when the children are a bit older, but the same principle can be used on any issue upon which you and your partner agree to disagree.

It is important to present a unified front to your child, even if you do not always agree on everything. When you present a unified front, you lessen the chance of your child rebelling in the future; you show him that he will not succeed in dividing you and your spouse.

When a child realizes that he is outnumbered and that his parents are sticking together no matter what, the child will begin to fall into line more quickly and is less likely to push his limits.

Chapter 10

5 Ways First Time or Frustrating Parents Should Handle Toddlers having Tantrums

Several licensed psychologists have confirmed the fact that toddler tantrum both at home and in the public places is just a normal thing. When a child demands something, and you are not able to give it to him or her, she may decide to show her frustration by throwing a tantrum. First-time parents should always be prepared for toddler tantrum and never get scared of it whether at home or in public. Sometimes your toddler may desire to have something you know he or she does not need.You should not for fear of tantrum give your child what he or she does not require. Rather you should be ready to accept the fact that the child can always calm down after some time of tantrum. Finding a way to avoid a tantrum, by all means, can make the child to always use that as a weapon against you when he or she wants to get something. So, the best thing is to only give her what she requires and never try to bribe her out of tantrum for any reason. Parents that always bribe their toddlers out of tantrum usually keep on bribing till the child has a wrong believe about life thinking that he or she can get anything by showing violence or displaying temper tantrum.

In chapter two of this Ebook, we introduced eight steps in helping toddlers come out of a tantrum. But, in this chapter we are going to talk about five ways first time or frustrating parents should use to handle toddlers having a tantrum. The reason for this is that most first time or frustrated parents usually find it difficult to control their emotions when their toddler is in the middle of a tantrum. For that reason, they usually elongate the issue or even intensify their toddler tantrum through their own meltdown. Some of them even usually go as far as flogging their toddlers, some even use screaming, whining and others. The problem with this is that toddlers normally learn very fast from their parents and can use what they learn against their parents. Parents are the first role models of their children who are constantly looking and monitoring their behaviors. You must know that your child is observing your actions, responses, your body language and others than your words even while they are in the middle of a tantrum.

Five ways first time or frustrated parents should use to handle toddlers having a tantrum are:

1.Stop whining and screaming at toddler: Most first time or frustrated parents usually think that screaming, whining or even lashing a child can help calm the tantrum. What they forget is that children usually get used to things easily and when they do, the thing will become entertaining to them. Some toddlers usually like to do something that will make their parent or minder scream or shout on top of their voice. But, there are some that always get scared easily and do not even need the screaming at all. But, whichever way, screaming at a toddler is never a good way of handling toddler tantrum. If care is not taken, you can even get into your own tantrum in the process of trying to command or force your toddler out of a tantrum. For that reason, you should never scream, yell, or even lash at them as that can result to a more embarrassing scene.

2.Try to ignore them completely: One of the ways to identify first-time parents is usually the manner in which they handle tantrum toddler. I have even once sighted a first-time mother that burst out in tears in a grocery store simply because of the embarrassment and frustration she felt as a result of her tantrum toddler. It is even more pitiful for you to know that even your cry and scream will not even make the toddler get out of the tantrum quicker. The most effective and efficient way to handle tantrum toddler is to ignore him or her completely. Do as if you do not recognize the frustration and the feeling that triggered the tantrum and he or she will come to you for consolation. This is simply the time you will need to show your compassion and care for her, which will end the whole embarrassment.

3. Offer rest or food to the toddler: Toddlers always get into a tantrum for several reasons including frustration as a result of hunger, tiredness, and others. It is your duty as a first-time parent to take time to study your toddler so as to know how he or she behaves while hungry or feeling sleepy. Some toddlers usually get into tantrum before they fall asleep and this is mostly as a result of negligence and lack of attention from the parent or minder. So, try as much as possible to see to it that your toddler has proper sleep time and feed appropriately. That can reduce the risk of a tantrum by more than 70%.

4.Give your toddler options, when possible: Toddlers love to take their own decision just as adults do. So, when you deny them the right to decide on what they want like the cloth to wear, the shoe to wear, the things to eat and others then you are the one that causes their tantrum. That does not mean you should allow your toddler to wear rag while going to church or other place with you. There are other better ways, and that include bringing out several clothes and good shoes for her to select. You will be surprised how excited your toddler will be after you finish doing that.

5.Introduce a countdown: You should always have it at the back of your mind that your toddler wants to be in control to an extent. So, moving from one activity to another without pre-informing her can make her throw a tantrum. By the time you introduced countdown, the toddler will already know what is coming next and prepare her mind for it. You can tell your toddler what the next activity is going to be and the one that follows that. That can be like "5 more cloths to eat launch", four more minutes to bedtime and others.

5 Areas To Address On Physical, Emotional, Relational, Spiritual, Cognitive And Behavioral Symptoms Of Stress For Parenting As A Result Of Toddler Tantrum

The effect of toddler tantrum to parents cannot be overstated. These always show in different areas of parent's life and mostly the first time parents. It does affect their physical, emotional, relational, spiritual, cognitive and even behavioral aspect of their lives. The reason for the stress is mostly due to the fact that parents often take it as their responsibility to make their toddlers behave the way they want them to behave which is not an easy thing to do. First-time parents should know that toddlers also have their own mind and thinking and will always like to do things their own way. For that reason, the more you try to force them into seeing things your way or behaving in a particular way the more they throw a tantrum to disgrace you in public. You will always stretch your emotion and lose when you think that you have the power to control a toddler completely.

There are some symptoms of stress for parenting as a result of a toddler tantrum. The symptoms can manifest in the physical form where everyone around will start asking you whether you are sick due to your look. You may end up growing thin and lose weight abnormally owing to the stress caused by toddler tantrum. While that is among the sacrifices made in parenting, there is always a way to reduce and diminish that from taking place, and that is by following the solutions provided in this book. More so, the physical symptom of stress for parenting as a result of toddler tantrum can result to sudden ailment like shortage of blood and other related issues.

The 5 Areas to address on symptoms of stress for parenting as a result of toddler tantrum include:

Managing physical and emotional stress: Parenting comes with lots of challenges and toddler tantrum is just one of them. Having a good understanding of toddler tantrum will make it easy for a parent to manage the emotional and physical stress it does come with. If your emotion is stressed, your physical outlook will show that, and it will transfer into your overall health. That is why first-time parents are advised to simply understand toddler tantrum as a normal development for their child and that it will soon be gone as the years go by.

Relational symptoms of parenting stress: Another area parenting stress as a result of toddler tantrum usually surface, is in the relationship of the parents with each other and other people around. Some parents find it difficult to enjoy each other's presence owing to the annoyance and embarrassment the child keeps on bringing to them while in the middle of a tantrum. Majority of first-time parents even do not relate fine with people around them. This is mostly due to quick judgment they usually get from people around them when their toddler misbehaves in public. It is true that people around your home, in public or others will judge you wrongly, but you have to try as much as you can to preserve your mind from outburst due to anger, and you will maintain your relationship with people around.

Cognitive symptoms of parenting stress: Someone who is emotionally and physically stressed will find it difficult to learn new things. So, the cognitive symptom is another sign of stress parents normally have as a result of a toddler tantrum. You can easily handle this by not expecting tantrums to go away quick and make sure it does not disturb your mind again. By the time you train your mind towards the frustration and annoyance caused by toddler tantrum, you will begin to recover your mental ability. Another thing to do in order to avoid affecting your learning ability through stress caused by a toddler tantrum is to always have a plan on what to do when your toddler throws a tantrum. Make sure you stick to the plan, and you will not have reason to worry about the toddler tantrum next time you are going out with her.

Behavioral symptoms of toddler stress: First-time parents usually end up behaving wrongly while their toddler is in the middle of tantrum without knowing. Some of them even usually get mad at anyone that judges them unfairly or quickly. In order to address this, you have to start applying a sense of humor which will make people never to notice your change in behavior as a result of your toddler tantrum. Also, you can easily control your actions and behavior when you stop thinking about tantrums and the frustration it is causing you. Just see it as the normal thing every child does and it will not cause much stress that will result to change in your behavior with time.

Spiritual symptoms of parenting stress: Parenting stress as a result of toddler tantrums can make one unable to pray and commune with his or her God. If your toddler throws a tantrum while you are in a religious gathering, you will no longer concentrate due to the feeling of anger, frustration, and embarrassment. You can still handle this by ignoring the child and people around knowing that toddlers are bound to throw a tantrum anywhere and at any time. But, ignoring your child in the middle of a tantrum is always easier to say than done especially by first-time parents.

Chapter 11: How Do You Discipline A Toddler?

Disciplining a toddler is an area that should be handled carefully. More often than not, toddlers are either over disciplined or under disciplined because parents do not always understand how the inner workings of a child's brain corresponds with the outer influences of their life. A toddler needs a variation of discipline levels in order for him or her to completely understand the issue or issues at hand. Over the next few paragraphs, we are going to discuss many facets of the child's behavior, the child's mind, and the influence that the parents have on the child. Yes, I did say the influence of the parent(s) as well.

Consistency

One of the first aspects that need to be taken into consideration is the fact that children need consistency. If a child is not supposed to stand on a chair, enforce that rule every time that it is broken. A child cannot learn what is right and wrong if the rules are bent or broken under some circumstances and enforced under other circumstances. Being the one to always enforce the rules may be hard, may make you feel like the bad guy, may even make you feel like you are over punishing, but it is also the only way that the child will learn that some things are acceptable, while others are not.

What is Worth the Fight

Do you remember what I said about consistency? Now, you take that and add to it that you must pick your battles. Is it really worth fighting over standing on the chair, running down the hallway, or playing in the sink while in the bathroom? Do you want to be constantly nagging your child over everything? Most parents have rules that they want their children to abide by, but you have to help the child develop a little at a time. Do not overdo it so that every time you speak to your child it is about something that he or she is not doing to your standards.

When a child constantly hears what they are doing wrong, it leaves little room in their minds to be able to realize all of the things that he or she does right. Set a couple rules, and see them through. Make sure the child knows that the rules are in place. Only at this point should you move forward and begin to enforce new rules. Also, lead by example. If the child is not supposed to slam doors, you shouldn't either. Children do what they are shown, and learn from those surrounding them.

Keeping that in mind, one must also realize that discipline is not always about punishment and wrong-doings. Children also learn what is right and what is wrong by praise. When he puts the cap back on the toothpaste, let him know that you are proud of him and happy that he remembered. When children see only discipline and punishment, they begin to think that is all there is. Let the child know that when they do good, good things happen. A star chart is a great way to help a child know that they have done something good.

Time-Out

When all of the praise and "mommy looks" do not get the job done, parents must resort to actual discipline. Toddlers should, under no circumstances, be spanked. Spankings tend to teach children that it is just fine to use violence to right their wrongs. Instead of spankings, use more subtle methods of discipline. An age-old tradition for "naughty" children is placing them in time-out. Time-out is a great way to pull the child away from an activity and give him/her a little time to calm down and think about what he or she did. Time-out can be very helpful, but when used incorrectly can also be very damaging.

When using time-out as a method of discipline, one should always use the "age to minute" method. This is when you place a child in time-out for only the amount of minutes that he or she is old. For instance, a four year old should be in time-out for four minutes and a three year old for three minutes. Before placing the child in time-out, you explain what he or she did wrong. After the child has completed the allotted time, you then make the child tell you why he or she was in time-out. By doing this, you are ensuring that the child knows why he or she is being punished.

Parents around the world are always learning to discipline their children as to what best suits their needs. The basic rules will always be there, no matter what culture or region you are from. While discipline is a very important role in a toddler's life, praise is as well. Always remember that your child is a model of you. Children mimic the environment in which they are surrounded. If you want your child to do something, you do it too.

Always set an example and be concise about what is expected and what will happen if it is not done. Always remember that children look to their peers and their parent(s)/guardian(s) for leadership, and if that leadership is not given in a healthy manor, the child will definitely act out. Children need attention, care, consistency, and schedules. To cut out any of these, would be cutting out a vital function in the child's development, thus stunting the child's brain.

Remember, the key to success is whatever you make it. The key to proper discipline is that the child never feels unwanted, unnecessary, or un-loved, but that the child still acknowledges and demonstrates what is right and wrong. Pique their interests, occupy their minds, and instill knowledge into them, which is what one must remember when handling children. They may be resilient, but they are also extremely fragile. Take care and caution when disciplining, think before you act, and most importantly, always show that you care.

Chapter 12: Childhood Worries And Anxiety

Childhood worries and anxiety can be a challenge for many parents. While children don't pay the bills, provide for the family, or manage the house, children have their share of daily demands and experiences that can lead to frustrations and disappointments. When this happens, children can get worried or stressed. Luckily, you can help your child to learn to manage stress and deal with everyday issues with ease. Having the ability to manage worries and anxiety successfully will help your child master life's challenges and setbacks, both big and small.

Understanding Childhood Worries and Anxiety

Every child experiences fears and anxiety from time to time, as they go through their different development stages. Your child may worry about (still) wetting the bed, failing a test, speaking up in class, the ball she/he missed while playing rugby, not having the latest shoes, missing the school bus or whether you will punish them for being disobedient, among many other things. Some of the signs and symptoms of childhood worries and anxiety can include:

- **Headaches**
- Stomach aches
- **Clinginess**
- **Restlessness**
- Excessive worries
- Sleep problems
- Impulsiveness
- Sweaty palms
- Nervous movement/twitches
- Difficulty in focusing or concentrating
- Muscle tension
- Accelerated heart rate as well as breathing

By encouraging your child to speak with you, together you can work on overcoming their fears and worries. Taking part in extracurricular activities is encouraged and help them to understand that things won't always go their way. Also, encourage your child to eat a balanced diet, move their body with exercise, and to get a good night's sleep. You can also help to plan their day and provide tips on how your child can deal with change if things don't go as planned. Children benefit from being flexible and being able to adapt easily to change. Finally, you should not forget to be their one true cheerleader, the person who encourages them in every way possible.

How to Talk to Your Child about What They Are Feeling

To help your child conquer worry and anxiety, you will need to communicate with them in a language that they understand. Children have a desire to be heard and understood, just as we do. There are certain ways that you can help your child to overcome worry:

- Be available. If you would like to know what is going on in your child's mind, it's important to be ready when they want to connect. Make sure you demonstrate that you are listening by using eye contact, displaying appropriate body language, e.g., stop cooking and sit with your child, and ensure you don't interrupt. Don't speak until they have finished talking.Sharing their stories can help children ease their fears and anxiety.
- Be empathetic. When your child opens up, don't be quick to dismiss their worry. What may seem small and unimportant to you, is often huge for your child. Tell them you understand their situation.
- Become solutions focused. When your child tells you about their problem, offer to help them deal with their issue constructively. Try brainstorming some positive alternative ways to look at the problem together, and discuss worst case scenarios. As tempting as it is, do not solve their problem for them. By children

participating actively in solving their problems, they can learn how to tackle issues independently.

• Reassure your child. Sometimes, when a child is troubled, all they need to move past their troubles is the reassurance from a loved one. Giving them a big hug or offering words of encouragement can go a long way. Reassuring your child of your unconditional support enables them to know that whatever happens, you will be there.

Teach your child the value of love, gratitude, fun, relaxation, mindfulness and enjoyment, as this can help children offset stress and perform well. Let your child know that all problems are only temporary and that they don't have to suffer alone. Remember, every problem has a possible solution!

Chapter 13: How Children Succeed

Parents often wonder if they are doing the right thing. "Should I do this? Should I say that?" The following steps will help you succeed in parenting.

Use Genuine Encounter Moments.

Your child's self-esteem is greatly influenced by the quality of time you spend with him. Not the amount of time. With our busy lives we are often thinking about the next thing that must be done instead of putting all your focused attention on what your child is trying to say. Don't ignore your child's attempt to communicate with you. Recognize that feelings are neither right nor wrong. They just are. So acknowledge what your child is saying to you about how he feels.

Use action and not words

According to statistics we give our children more than 2 000 compliance requests during a day! No wonder they sometimes switch off! So stop nagging your child about socks lying around. Only wash the socks that were in the washing basket and let your child experience the result. Action speaks louder than words.

Give children ways to feel powerful

If you don't do this, your child will find inappropriate ways to feel their power. Ways to help them feel powerful and valuable are to ask their advice, give them choices and let them help in the kitchen. We often do the job for them because we can do it with less hassle, but the result is that they feel unimportant.

Use natural consequences

Don't interfere in any situation. We rob our children of the chance to learn from the consequences of their actions. By allowing consequences to do the talking, we avoid disturbing our relationships by nagging or reminding too much. Allow them to find solutions and learn the importance of remembering.

Use logical consequences

The consequences are often too far in the future to practically use a natural consequence. In such a case, logical consequences are effective. A consequence for a child must be logically related to the behavior in order for it to work.

Withdraw from conflict

If your child is testing you through a tantrum or by being angry or speaking disrespectfully to you, leave the room or tell the child that you will be in the next room if he wants to 'try again'. Do not leave in anger or defeat.

Separate the deed from the one doing it

Never tell the child that he is bad. That is bad for his self-esteem. Rather tell the child that you do not like what he **did**. He must know you love him unconditionally no matter what he does. Do not motivate your child by withdrawing your love from him.

Be kind and firm — all at once

If your child did something you don't approve of, reprimand him, but do it in a loving way. Do not motivate fear. Be strict and loving at the same time.

Keep the end in mind

We all want the situation under control as soon as possible. We are looking for the expedient solutions. This often results in children who feel overpowered. But if we parent in a way that keeps in mind how we want our child to be as a parent, we well be more thoughtful in the way we parent.

Be consistent and follow through

If you have made an agreement that your child cannot buy candy when she gets at the store, do not give in to her pleas, tears, demands or tantrums. Your child will learn to respect you more if you mean what you say.

Chapter 14: Taking Care Of The Children After A Divorce

It can be a frightening experience to think about how you will take care of your children after a divorce. There are going to be many changes and one of the parents will be making the most decisions and you need to be confident that you can make them. Sometime you maybe forced to have to turn to friends and family members for emotional and financial support so don't be too ashamed to take advantage of the help that is offered. In some cases you may just need some one to talk to about the divorce. It is also necessary to learn how to manage your financial budget which may result in cutting back on un-necessary expenses but in time everyone will be just fine as long as everyone's basic needs are being met. Parents should not worry about their children missing out on material things due to the financial limitations. Think of cost effective things you can do as a family. Most cities have lots of entertainment free or relatively cheap. In large cities there are impromptu concerts by street musicians or just sat in the park and people watch. Go to the matinee instead of going to the movies during primetime. If money gets extremely tight let the cable TV go and buy or rent movies. The computer is a great option for watching a TV show or movie. Take the kids to the local bookstore and hang out. In the summer, there is always a local food festival or street fair in most cities. Let the kids get involved in a community group, like a theatre.

Above all make sure there is open communication with your children after a divorce and ensure they are comfortable enough to come to you to talk about anything.While you may get emotional during some discussions you have to be strong. If you are positive about everything turning out fine they will believe in it as well. Both ex's should do their very best to get along with each other to make it possible to take care of the children. Divorced parents should try to focus on being strong for their children because it is extremely hard to go from a two parent household to one. When things begin to get overbearing don't be afraid to seek counseling for all of you if you feel it could be beneficial.

Children Of Various Ages Deal with Divorce Differently

Some parents divorce when their children are small so they don't remember them as a couple. There are other kids that remember that divorce and what took place.Children of different ages deal with divorce differently. Parents should be prepared to deal with the age variation. Some children may accept a simple explanation that one of the parents will not be living in the house. For others they see as an end to life as they know it. The parents should be prepared to understand the needs of the child and be prepared to discuss it. It is extremely important to try to understand the feelings of your children and how they are relating to the divorce. Even very young children can understand the emotions of people and often identify issues such as stress and tension. This may result in some type of behavior change. They may begin to cling to one or both of their parents and may experience temper tantrums as well spells of crying. Younger children may exhibit changes in their eating and sleeping patterns as well.

Children in range of three to five maybe able to ask general questions about the divorce because they become more aware that the other parent isn't around like they used to be. They maybe become inquisitive as to why the other parent doesn't go places with them like they use to.Children that fall within the age of around six to eleven will most likely have a better defined idea about what divorce means; however that does not mean that they are accepting it. Be prepared for possible changes in their behavior as well as some challenging questions.In fact children of this age group are simply overwhelmed with anger and it is openly displayed. The children that are considerably older in the range of twelve and up often understand more about divorce than any other age group and try to arrive at more detailed answers about the divorce. They are often aware of some issues in the marriage before the announcement of the divorce.

The parents should try to get the children to see both parents as equal and always present a united front.Both parents should try to handle their own emotions and never use children as a confidante, but instead turn to a trusted friend or even better a professional counselor. Always remember that the approach you take with your children during the divorce process is going to have an impact on them for the rest of their lives. With that in mind, try to have a civil relationship with the ex-spouse so the children will feel some sense of security.

Signs That Children May Not Be Coping Well With A Divorce

Divorce is very different in the eyes of children then adults. The transition to living in a single-parent family is difficult for kids. They may feel abandoned or insecure or may feel isolated and different from other kids. They don't always comprehend the reason for the divorce and you should not get too caught up in your own issues to notice what they need. Not every child is going to tell you what they are feeling and experiencing with the divorce.There are signs that will give you an indication they are having difficulty accepting the divorce. Many children exhibit signs of anxiety which causes them to have changes in their moods. They maybe fine one moment and in tears the next and also show signs of aggressions. There maybe changes in their eating habits and how well they sleep. You may notice an extreme change in appearance particularly for older children. They may stop paying attention to their personal hygiene and their choice of clothing and hairstyles may be drastically different from what would be considered normal. Parents may notice that the children simply withdraw and want to be along and not talk or deal with their feelings. Some children began to have difficulty in school, stop hanging out with their friends and don't engage in normal activities. This is a true indication they may be suffering from depression. It is difficult to inflict punish on your children when they are acting out due to the divorce; however, you must have boundaries and guidelines. They must be taught to deal with their feelings of anger in a positive way.

Open communication is the key to help discover how the children are coping with the divorce and move toward finding a positive outcome. As a parent you should use your own judgment to decide when intervention needs to take place. Keep in mind that there is no defined time frame as to when children will have issues dealing with their parent's divorce.

Chapter 15: What You Can Do To Ensure Healthy School Lunches Are Available To Your Children

Lunch is one of the most important meals of the day for children.After they have used up all the nutrients they received from breakfast, lunch is what powers them through the rest of the school day.Therefore, it is vitally important to provide your child with the best possible lunch, in order to give him/her the vitamins, minerals, and protein necessary to keep him/her focused in school and active after school. If your child's school provides lunch options, try to work with the school's administration to ensure that the healthiest options are offered.Tell them to avoid junk foods, especially fried foods, such as French fries, as well as meals that are loaded with fats and sugars, which only provide a spike of energy before dragging your child down harshly once the body regulates again.

If you are bagging a lunch for your child every day, you have much more control over what he/she eats, so take an extra few minutes out of every morning to put together a healthy meal.You want to provide protein and complex carbohydrates for energy, so foods like peanut butter, whole wheat bread, fruits, and vegetables work wonders.Provide a small bag of nuts, such as walnuts, almonds, or peanuts, as a snack as well, because they are loaded with healthy fats and protein.A salad of raw vegetables and dried or fresh fruits can provide abundant nutrients in their raw forms, which is the best way to derive the most energy.

The Effects of Involving Children in Extra-Curricular Activities for Physical Growth

Your child is required to wake up each day for school, but school can be quite stressful.Though your child may have plenty of friends, there is always the issue of peer pressure from those children he/she may not get along well with, and there is also a lot of pressure, from teachers and school administrators, to behave and perform well on classroom assignments and exams.Because school can be stressful, give your children the opportunity to do fun activities after school.

To provide your child with something to look forward to after school, consider involving him/her in extra-curricular activities that engage physical bodies as well as minds.Whether it is a school's chess club or soccer team, encourage your children to explore their likes and dislikes beyond the classroom, and to grow more and meet new people who may not be in their immediate circle or in the same grade.

You can also enroll your children in extra-curricular activities outside of the school system completely, such as gymnastics classes, dancing classes, or musical lessons. Your child will learn new skills and gain a very high sense of confidence, thanks to the newfound abilities he/she never thought were possible.

In addition, if a child is involved in musical lessons, for example, he/she will learn math skills in order to learn to keep time with the music and to read sheet music. If a child is involved on a sports team or in a dance group, he/she will learn how to work as a team member, developing skills that encourage caring about others on the team and working together to succeed as opposed to working against each other.

Chapter 16: Parenting Styles And Diana Baumrind Theory

Diana Baumrind developed a very famous theory in 1960. This theory is based on three styles of parenting. These are named "authoritative, permissive and authoritarian". Later, another important factor has been added by Maccoby and Martin called uninvolved. Diana was very successful and well accepted to study more than 100 preschoolers. With a series of observations and interviews with parents and other research methods using naturalistic observation, Diana was able to do all this. This helped her to recognize and understand four important aspects of parenting, including expectation of control and maturity, communication styles, warmth and nurturance, and disciplinary strategies. The three basic types of theory were based on these dimensions.

Depending on the style of authoritarian parents, children are expected to strictly follow the regulations and rules established by them. When the children are not able to meet the rules, parents tend to punish. Authoritarian parents are unable to provide an explanation on the rules established. If a child needs an explanation, the answer is simple: "Because I said so." Usually, these parents have high expectations and demands and are less responsive (Baumrind, 2005). These parents, according to Baumrind are "obedience- and status-oriented, and expect their orders to be obeyed without explanation". Children are expected to fully respond to these parents and they do not tolerate the rules and regulations established by them. Although, they are less interactive with their children but they expect children to be matured. The children of these parents tend to concentrate on their studies and tend to have good grades. Negative effect of authoritarian parenting is that children cannot develop a social behavior because they are not encouraged motivated to develop and provide opinions. They lack decision making power and are unconfident and shy. They become less interactive by this and it also influences their decisions. Following figure shows the authoritarian parenting style.

Figure 3: Authoritarian Parenting

Authoritative parenting is the second parenting style. This is relatively a democratic parenting style; parents are sensitive and responsive to their children. Usually, they prefer to answer their children's questions (Baumrind, 2013). They are also very encouraging and like to forgive rather punishing the child. It is suggested by Baumrind that these parents "monitor and communicate clear standards for their children's conduct. They are forceful, but not aggressive and restrictive". They adopt supportive methods. They want the child to be safe and socially responsible. Children in this style are able to develop personal opinions. Children of these parents are socially interactive and reliable. Following figure shows the authoritative parenting style.

Figure 4: Authoritative Parenting

Baumrind's third parenting style is permissive parenting. These parents often refer to the tolerant parents and they are less demanding with their children. "As they have lower expectations of maturity and self-control, these parents are concerned less about disciplining the children" (Baumrind, 1991). According to Baumrind, "permissive parents are more receptive than demanding. They are less concerned about culture and are soft. They do not require mature attitude, allow significant self-regulation, and avoid conflict" (Baumrind, 1991). They are kind to their children and are friends of them. Communication between parents and children in this style is encouraged. Permissive parents' children have developed lower levels of depression, social skills, and confidence. A positive and optimistic human posture is developed by these factors.Negative impact of permissive parenting is that emotional development of child doesn't grow and hence is damaged. Following figure shows the permissive parenting style.

Figure 5: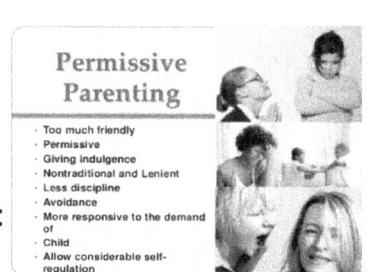

Permissive Parenting

Uninvolved parenting is the last category added by Maccoby and Martin. Generally, these parents are less reactive, less communicative, and less demanding. They are able to meet basic needs and the needs of their children, but they usually don't have much attachment with their children. These parents, in some cases, are so ignorant that they sometime ignore the basic needs of their children. These parents are ambivalent to the desires and needs of their children. They are ignored by their children. Parents are less demanding, and there are rules designed for their children, such as children without praise, encouragement, and communication. These parents' children lack confidence and develop some negative personality traits (Hughes, et al., 2005). They are not socially active and reliable, due to low demand is met by parents to avoid social growth. They are not educated to handle different situations, thus it affects their cognitive development negatively.

There is a significant impact on child psychology of these parenting styles. The study of 100 preschoolers helped in developing a crust impact on children of the parenting. For example, authoritarian style often used the obedient and respectful children who are still experts, but lower happiness scale and social skills. The result is opposite in authoritative parenting style as it results in socially capable and happy children. In permissive parenting children often face problems courageously and often have low or weak school performance. Finally, uninvolved parenting has the lowest ranking among all styles of parenting. These children grow as individuals with fewer skills and qualification, low self-esteem, and less self-control because they are neglected by their parents.

"Another important aspect of education is that teenage behavior is an important step that can have a significant impact on economic growth (Querido, Warner, and Eyberg, 2002)". For example, if a child violates curfew, both parents take steps to treat children of implementing measures. Along these lines, the kid's conduct impacts the style received by parents. A helpful and inspired kid will probably have parents who adopt an attitude of parents with authorities. A careless, immature, and unhelpful teen, on the other hand, might be expected by other parenting styles like uninvolved and authoritarian parenting style. Parents change their habits of parenting with time. Some parents are less rigid younger children and more rigid with elder ones. Therefore, changes in culture and environment, change how parents and parenting.

Ethnicity is another important aspect that can affect parents. It was found that parental authority is common for white families than others. Moreover, the authoritative parenting style seems more common in families of ethnic minorities. Impact of culture and beliefs of the parents is the basic reason behind this. For example, families of ethnic minorities generally live in the area where life is dangerous due to dangerous neighborhood; it is necessary for parents to behave as authoritarian for their children's life safety. There are other measures that can affect the way parenting style is. For example, external factors, such as the human personality and theattitude of child, and stress at work, also internal factors such as mood and lack of sleep. All these factors play an important role in the style matrix approved by parents.

According to different styles of parenting study, authoritative parenting is considered as the most efficient, productive and beneficial to children compared with the other three parenting styles. The answer to the question that why authoritative parenting is best is that there are several reasons that can be classified as "warm and receptive attitude of parents towards their children in a comfortable home. Because of this comfortable home, children often develop a positive approach to life (Amato, and Fowler, 2002)". Authoritative style parenting children tend to be autonomous, content and self-controlled, therefore, have a positive attitude in general. They develop to interact with peers efficiently and effectively and have personal opinion. They are able to handle the situation in a rational manner.

Overall culture and surrounding can have a fundamental effect on the parenting style. "Research has shown that most Chinese parents adopt authoritarian parenting style". "Chinese parents are strict about rules and regulations; freedom is not given to Chinese children and parents are usually strict. One of the main reasons for this parenting style is the child policy imposed by the government which restricts all Chinese families to have only one child (Zimmerman and Schunk, 2011)". As a result of this policy, Chinese parents focus all the attention on the only child. It leaves no room for error on the part of parents. "Thus the parenting style of China is similar to the authoritarian style of Diana Baumrind's theory of parenting".

In general, every parenting style influences the behavior of children. Parents have parental inconsistency in behavior which can be dangerous for children. None of parenting styles is absolutely right or absolutely wrong. It's a continuous job and should be developed in a timely manner to new circumstances and situations. "The results are never 100 percent". Raising children refers to where how we were raised, when we were raised, and we were raised. "All these factors play an important role in the matrix". The attitude and behavior of children should be constantly monitored and style of parenting should be changed accordingly. Rigidity is never wise in parenting.

Chapter 17: Crafting With Kids

Most children love to do craft projects, and this can be a fun way to teach them new things.There are endless possibilities to how you can do this.Begin gathering supplies that they can use when they would like to.Here are a few suggestions. Start collecting objects that can be reused.Small baby food containers, empty toilet rolls, twist ties from bread bags, small cardboard boxes, and old birthday cards are some ideas.Put them in a box with some markers, glue, scissors, and heavy cardstock and let your child's imagination flow. Teach them about volcanoes and then make a volcano from clay or playdough.You can make a playdough that you can dry, or simply reuse when finished.

Or get some paint and paper and create a volcano through painting.Volcanoes are just one idea; you could use any subject to teach through crafts.Scrapbooking is a fun activity with kids and can be really simple.Find some items that they can add to a scrapbook, like the confetti from their birthday party, the cards they received, and a balloon.Use these objects to decorate the scrapbook page and include the pictures from their party.Show them how to journal to help them record their thoughts from that event.

Make a craft box with different types of crafts they can use.Include paper, markers, crayons, paints, glues, tape, wood sticks, and other items.Back to school sales are a great time to stock up on some of these supplies.Allowing your kids to create with crafts gives them an outlet for the creativity that we want to bloom inside.Make sure you marvel at their creation, and they will love you for it.

Disciplining for each Child

There are many books with varying opinions on how you should discipline your children.However, I believe that the person that knows your child best is you.Articles and books can give advice, but it is important to understand your child and what will work for them. Not all children are the same, and this applies to children in the same family.Using time out for one child may not work for another.It's important to understand this and not try to force the same discipline on a child that it won't work for.

A friend of mine has a child who defies all the rules of discipline and parenting.He had a problem biting and she asked me for advice.I told her every method I have ever heard of to stop a child from biting, and she had tried them all.She had to take the time to understand him and find out what works for him.Disciplining children is important.They need to understand that there are rules, and when they break the rules, there are consequences.

However, understandably, the discipline should not use force that could be harmful to the child.When properly disciplined, a child will learn tools that will help them throughout their lives.The discipline should also relate to the act.If a child colors all over a wall, they should have to clean up the mess.If they are too small, give them some time to try alone and then help them.Make sure it isn't a game to them, they need to understand that they are in trouble.Understanding your child and finding out what discipline works for them will help them become well adjusted as they get older, and help your household to run smoother.

Healthy Eating for Kids

Chicken nuggets and macaroni and cheese seem to be the mainstream diet for many children.Parents often struggle to get their children to eat healthy foods.Our family started on a new diet.We switched our white bread for wheat and started stocking the fridge with fruits and vegetables.The kids rebelled for a while, but now they are used to it.They fight for the last strawberry.Here are some suggestions to help you make the transition to healthy eating in your home.Monitor how many snacks your children eat in a day.The rule at our house is a snack at 10:00 a.m. and 3:00 p.m.I don't have whiny kids wanting treats all day, because they know when they can have them.

However, if they want something healthy like an apple, a bagel, or some fruit, they can have it without asking.Add more vegetables to the dinner table.Try a variety of vegetables, and keep trying them even when your kids say they don't like them.Taste buds change over time.Have them try one bite each time you serve something they don't like.

Make food more fun.Serving dinner that your kids can adapt to their own tastes makes dinner more fun, and gets them to eat better.Try taco soup with a base to include tomatoes and pinto beans and let them add their own ingredients: cheese, sour cream, chips, olives, corn, etc.They probably won't notice that there were tomatoes in there.Healthy eating takes time but is worth it in the end.Your kids will adjust and eventually won't miss the candy and chips that they used to munch on.And everyone will benefit from the change.

Chapter 18: Tips For Building Happiness

We often think that our circumstances i.e. where we live, what we have, what we earn and so on have a big effect on how happy we are. However, these things tend to have much less impact than most people expect. Research suggests the greatest determinant of our happiness is usually our attitude and personal choices as opposed to our circumstances. So many things in life make us happy:playing at the park, bubble baths, dessert, presents, a good movie etc. Apart from these, I also noted that friends and family both have a profound impact on your child. Helping your child discover their personal strengths and helping them to improve them is a great way to create happiness. When your child tries doing something frequently but are unable to do the task, they are usually very happy when they finally are able to do it. These small things are what makes your child happy.

Additionally, by helping your child see what their unique gifts are, you can also encourage them to use those strengths to help others in creative, meaningful ways. Below are some essential tips for building happiness.

Show Gratitude

Each day that we can breathe is a blessing. There are so many other things to be thankful for in our environment. Express your gratitude regularly by using words like, "thank you," "you are welcome" and make a point to tell your children why you do so. In order to create happiness in your children, encourage them to look around and be thankful for at least three things each day. They can be thankful for the pet they have, breakfast, and their school teacher and so on. To be grateful is also much more than saying "thank you." A grateful child is much happier, healthier and has feeling of fulfillment than a sad child. For instance, children who are sad usually cry a lot ending up even more sad and depressed. By helping your child to focus on the positive things in life, they will still find a way to be happy even when they don't get into the football team or don't pass their tests as they would have expected.

Provide For Basic Needs

Researchers have found that having your basic needs met, such as food, shelter, and clothing creates high levels of long-term satisfaction in people. Truth be told, without one of the basic needs stated, you cannot feel whole and this means your happiness will also be minimal. An adult is able to have self-control and immediate understanding but for a child, they will cry when they lack food and demand for it. As a parent, you should put your child's basic needs as a first priority. Even when you are going through a hard time as a family, you should strive to provide basic needs to your child. For instance most children feel sad andrefuse to go to school when they have nothing to carry for lunch as they will feel awkward surrounded by other children who have carried packed lunch. Therefore, to create happiness for your child, basic needs are so significant.

Appreciate Simplicity

It is the simple things in life that matter. It might take some time to actually stop and teach our kids to appreciate the simple things, but living in the present moment and focusing on the small and simple things can really do quite a boost for our appreciation, gratitude, and level of peace and well-being. Appreciating things that are around us brings us much happiness than when you are always complaining. I would advise that you start showing your child how each and every thing that is around them contributes to their happiness. For example, flowers are able to brighten up the environment and give you peace of mind. Let them appreciate the beautiful blue sky and the wonderful snow during winter. Teach your children to appreciate the sunlight and the fresh air.

These things may seem simple and trivial but just imagine if there was no sunlight, how would life be?

Do Activities Together

Happiness comes with fun. Participation in different kinds of activities will boost both your mood and that of your child, which will definitely increase happiness in the home. Engage in sports together, some volunteer work, competitions and other activities. Trust me, children love the time they spend with their parents more than anything. During this time, just plan to enjoy and have a nice time and not to start discussing about how your child wronged you unless of course they bring the topic up. You will be surprised that you will also feel rejuvenated and happy after spending some quality time with your child.

Create A Healthy Environment

The environment in which a child grows up will to a large extent determine their happiness. If you are the kind of parent who is always giving orders, and never have time to listen to your children and have some fun, then there is a very high likelihood that you will have unhappy children. In addition, constant fights with your spouse are not the best environment for your child. Many studies have shown how the relationship with your spouse positively or negatively affects your children. Therefore, if you are looking to have happy children be careful how you relate with not only your spouse but other people around you. Your child needs to see love in how you interact with them as well as how you interact with other people.

Give Space For Growth

Each one of us needs some air to breathe and a little space to ourselves. At times, children go through a lot of stress and experience fatigue too. When they do so, they need the space to be able to sort out their own issues. This is your first lesson on giving space. Just as you feel a great need to walk back after an exhausting shopping, your child needs space too. Space is required to breathe, to think, reason and enjoy. Children require space too but mostly are surrounded with supervisors and hence lack expression. Allow them some free time so that they can be themselves and not to always supervise them all the time. Happiness is not something that can be given or taught; a child needs that space to be able to acquire and show happiness even in the worst of situations.

Chapter 19: The Bomb Site Bedroom

There is something magnetic about teenage knickers that make them stick to the carpet and stay there for around five years.

Kids who go through an angelic childhood and who rarely step out of line have been known to drive their parents to drink when they reach their teens (the kids not the parents!)Keeping a bedroom clean and tidy is a small thing to parents whose job it is to keep the whole of the rest of the house in shape.Sadly, kids don't see it this way and most homes go through a stage where the top floor resembles London's East End three days into the Blitz.

And nothing you do seems to work right?You can ask, you can reason, you can plead and you can beg but all you will get are promises to do better and the next day the mess is still there...

Of course it would not be quite so infuriating if the mess was contained solely within the domain of the pseudo vampire on the top floor but invariably half the kitchen plates and glasses are locked away behind an impregnable wall of teenage angst with one of those hotel 'Do Not Disturb' cardboard hangers on the door knob...

Exact Programming is something that has been tried and works – well – sort of – but only to a degree.Exact Programming is when you tell your teenager **exactly** what to do without leaving a margin for alternatives.For instance:'Please take all of the dirty cups, glasses and plates from your bedroom and put them upstairs.'

Now this request sounds fair enough but in fact has two errors:Firstly you did not specify **where** upstairs, which will result in the dirty dishes being deposited at the top step of the main staircase.Secondly you forgot to include the word 'laundry' so you will have the crockery back but the dirty laundry will stay where it is.Exact Programming could alter teenage behaviour for at least ten minutes – until the next unsociable issue arises anyway!

The Privacy Issue

Teenagers take their privacy seriously and for concerned parents this is a bit of a No Man's Land – you want your teenager to learn the value of respecting other people's space but at the same time you would like to be able to invade theirs so you can be assured they are not on drugs, becoming dependent on alcohol or in an abusive relationship.

Certainly there are areas of a child's life as they hit their teenage years when they must be given a certain amount of freedom to explore their own friendships, make their own decisions – however badly they might turn out – and general 'learn the hard way'. The trick is to try not to 'lose touch' with your child (and your child will remain your child until they are well into their forties!)

There is a delicate line that is drawn where your child will turn to you for friendship and advice and a no-go zone reserved for interaction with kids of their own age – this area of knowledge features a list of misdemeanours they are not particularly proud of and won't want you to know about...

It is vital to know where this line is.It is also advisable **not** to step over it.You can be frantic with worry and deeply concerned about something you think your child is keeping from you but if you overstep that line you will find it almost impossible to win your child's confidence back...

Overstepping the line includes actions such as reading diaries, reading letters, telephoning mothers of other friends to find out information, searching private drawers and lockers and school bags and pockets... you get the general idea right?In fact many youngsters write their diary in a fantasist's world and much of the content is simply the scribblings of the person the child would **like** to be.Viewing such material as an accurate portrayal of what your child is doing and thinking in the real world is therefore misleading.

If there is something bothering you and you want to know – try asking.This might result in a tantrum but at least you tried.Start by stating that you have not been snooping because you don't believe that would be fair BUT...Often your kid will appreciate you did not invade a private area and share a confidence with you.If not, try again another time...

The importance of respect, privacy and also give and take is a lesson all parents should at least try to pass to their kids but surprisingly few young people reach their twenties with a decent grounding in civilities.

Rebellion

It happens to all kids – it arrives along with pubic hair and heavy metal.At some stage between Barbie dolls and wedding bells your kid will morph into an unrecognisable monster with selective amnesia.And of course the difficulty in dealing with rebellion is that the whole point of rebellion is to counter whatever the significant adult in your life is trying to impress upon you!

Kids going through puberty have a lot to contend with. Boys suffer the humiliation of still sporting a squeaky voice and still being able to manage a creditable soprano for the school choir when it seems to them that all their friends are knee-deep in women and shaving twice a day...Boys in their early teens can be gangly, pimply, plagued with growing pains, constantly hungry and full of agony because the girl they have fallen in love with is fawning all over the local football hero.

Girls tend to take comfort in large groups of friends – usually picking out one special 'lifelong' buddy they will stick with through thick and thin, regardless of how unsuitable that friend might be...Period pains, spots, fizzy hair, puppy fat... for girls the problems are different but no less stressful.

In the angst gaps, which seemingly occur about twice a month, your kid re-emerges and puts his arms around you or plops a wet kiss on your cheek...Fitful displays of affection are usually followed by a request for money but hey you can't have everything!

As with most crises throughout childhood and teens the best way to deal with rebellion is with complete calm.Yelling achieves nothing and can make things infinitely worse.Shouting and screaming that homework has not been done or rooms have not been cleaned simply conveys the message that it is acceptable to shout and scream and that is all that will happen – more shouting and screaming...Take a step back, draw breath and try another approach.

There are no guarantees that a soft approach will succeed either but what is certain is that it will at least help retain a level of respect between you and your monster.

An absolute no-no is the 'I am washing my hands of you' nonsense.This is simply a selfish desire to walk away from someone who has become too much trouble and too hot to handle.Walking away would be nice but you know in your heart it is going to make everything spectacularly worse so don't do it.

Teenagers tend to bring home ghastly friends with equally ghastly habits.Having taught your kid to embrace all cultures and all walks of society it seems a little churlish to start criticising people who want to eat with their hands or smoke in your kitchen.A pretty good yardstick to go by is to ask yourself whether you would accept this behaviour, whatever that behaviour might be, from an adult guest – if you would not, put a stop to it by politely requesting (not demanding) they stop/go home/ leave/ - whatever...And don't accept refusals.Be softly spoken about it but resolved.

Throughout the adolescent years it is so important to retain affection.By the end of the nineteenth year of aggravation and wanting to put your kid's head through the nearest window you will see an old pattern emerge – the twelve-year-old you loved comes shining through.Alternatively they might disappear on a two-year hike through Thailand and neglect to contact you for months on end just to add a few more grey hairs to your already bleach-white head!

Thinking back to your own teenage years and remembering how it felt to be constantly nagged and told how to live your life can be tedious and unhelpful. Few people lived an exemplary teenage life and fathers remembering their years as a stud muffin tend to cling even closer to precious daughters!Teenagers are human too, which brings us to another area of concern…

Chapter 20: Helping Your Child Embrace Individuality

The next step in helping your child unleash his or her inner power is to help your child accept who he or she is, as well as accept his or her uniqueness. Doing this helps your child in numerous ways.

First, it helps your child embrace his or her individuality and become content with whoever they are. Secondly, it helps your child realize that he or she is different and special in his or her own way; therefore, he or she should stop comparing him or herself to others.

Thirdly, when your child accepts him or herself, the child becomes courageous enough to become whoever he or she wants to be.

How To Help Your Child Embrace His Or Her Individuality

If you want your child to enjoy these benefits, help him or her admit his or her uniqueness along with all flaws and strengths. Here's how you can achieve this goal.

Do not be shy of being yourself: Start by having a talk that teaches your child the importance of being true to yourself. Tell your child that no harm comes from being truly unique. Therefore, your child should confidently be whom he or she is because this is what makes your child different from others. Tell your child how quirky you were as a child. Nevertheless, this did not stop you from portraying your true self because this is what makes you.

Moreover, teach your child that the secret to triumphing over the competition is to be different. The world craves for fresh and different things. To rule the world, you need to give the world precisely what it wants: **uniqueness.** This is why you need to confidently portray your true self. The more comfortable you become with yourself, the better you will be able to explore yourself and come up with novel ideas to maximize your capabilities.

Prevent peer pressure: Many children face peer pressure at school and the peer pressure keeps children from being their own self. Observe how your child feels and behaves after returning home from school, and keep a check on your child's academic performance. If you find your child feeling uncomfortable when you drop him or her off at school, or find your child's school grades dropping, it is probably due to peer pressure.

To help your child battle peer pressure, tell your child that it's okay to be unique and do you own thing; after all, everybody is different. Therefore, he or she should not be afraid of being whom he or she truly is. Additionally, you could also talk to your child's teachers to ensure your child is not falling prey to ridicule or criticism from other students.

Be comfortable in your own skin: In addition, teach your child to be comfortable in his or her own skin, and stop comparing him or herself to other children. So what if your daughter is not as thin or as tall as the popular girl in class is? Well, simple; your daughter has gorgeous eyes and should be proud of that. Help your child find out his or her strengths, beautiful physical features, and qualities so that your child knows that he or she has something to be happy about and can stop the comparison game.

Be the friend your child can confide in: To ensure that your child does not bottle his or her emotions, be a friend your child can confide in. Never judge, be critical of, or scrutinize your child. Instead, provide your child with a comforting shoulder to cry on. Your child needs to feel that you are his or her closest friend and confidant, and not enemy. Only then will your child share his or her feelings with you.

Let your child follow his or her dreams: Moreover, tell your child to dream as much as he or she can because dreams help your child become ambitious; ambition is essential to being successful.

Assure your child of your support irrespective of which career path your child wants to pursue and teach your child that he or she can be whoever he or she wants to be. When your child hears these things from you, the child understands that you want him or her to take control of his or her life, which will help the child feel independent and strong. This will help the child make mistakes, learn from them, have new experiences, and learn to make the right decisions.

Chapter 21: Make Time

There has been much ink spilled over the concept of quantity time versus quality time.The fact is that it is all time. If all you have because of work and things needing to be fixed around the house is fifteen minutes to just sit on the couch together, then give your kids that fifteen minutes on the couch.

If you are just waiting around for some mythical perfect time, you will be waiting a long time. The more you wait for the quality the less quantity you will have.Besides, there may never be a perfect time.All you can guarantee is the time you have right now so it is wise to make the best of it.

You also do not need to plan the world's greatest experiences either.You don't need to wait five months for the perfect set of hiking conditions to present themselves.Nor do you need to spend a ton of money.

You will find that often, the simplest and most memorable things that you can do are actually free. Some of the best times I've had with my own children are when we've made a lunch at home and gone to eat it in one of the local parks. Just hanging out and chatting about whatever.

If you have more than one child, making time will get harder, especially if there is a large age separation. They will just have different interests, maturity levels, and even their size differences can get in the way of easily doing something that everyone can enjoy.

My own kids range from twelve to one. So when we go to the beach it is impossible to just dive in and play in the water with the older kids and keep an eye on the youngest.

There are a couple of ways to solve those problems. One is to take turns with

your spouse. Trade-off who has to be the supervisor and who gets to play and get in on all the action. Hopefully no one will get burnt out and the kids will wind up getting time with both parents.

The other is to give them one-on-one time. What I've done is let them each pick a day where they get time with me. It isn't all day and it isn't necessarily whatever they want. For example, we can't afford to go out to eat and see a movie every day.

So we do simple things like read a book together, play Minecraft, tennis, or one of my daughters and I are even working on a children's story. Just be open to what they suggest and be prepared to offer your own, based on what you have seen their interests are.

I had to implement this because while I always try to give my kids attention and take time to listen, it becomes nearly impossible when they all want that attention at the same time.

Before long, no one gets any of my time and yet at the end of the evening, it was easy to feel frazzled and exhausted. This method ensures that at least one gets my undivided attention nearly every day.It also gives them something to look forward to and plan for throughout the week.

They are also less inclined to pepper me with questions and requests as soon as I come home from work, meaning that I am happier and less tired at the end of the day.

I'm not suggesting that you need to do the exact same thing.Find a method that works for you and your family.So long as it involves spending time and doing something together, then you are on the right track.

Chapter 22: The After Effects Of Divorce

Often, it's hard for adults to recognize just how many changes the divorce can bring into a child's life.Aside from the parents no longer being together, there are many intricacies within the world of the child that change.

While the husband and wife might be quite happy that they're no longer together and don't have to deal with each other as much, the child experiences a number of changes, concerns and worries.

For instance, there may be quite a difference in the number of activities the child can do after a parent moves out.Because of time constraints with one parent working more than they used to, many kids end up not being able to participate in extracurricular activities.

The family may also have less money to work with, and the one custodial parent may have less energy to do things.Arranging transportation may be a real issue unless there are close family and friends who can help out.

Often, after one parent moves out it means that the contact with a set of grandparents may lesson too.This can create a huge sense of loss for children.

Of course, some kids end up moving into a new home after the divorce.That means that they may have to go to a new child care facility or even a new school.They will certainly have to learn to make new friends within their neighborhood which can present a challenge as well.Kids are often embarrassed that their parents are divorced and may be jealous of their friends whose parents are still together.

The custodial parent may have to get a new or secondary job to make ends meet.Because of this, there may be less time that the child gets to spend with the custodial parent and the non-custodial parent.

Another change, albeit a good one, is that there may be less conflict and fighting in the home.Prior to divorce, there may have been consistent fighting between the parents.There may have been a lot of criticism going on between the parents.Often, this continues even after a divorce when parents end up in a custody battle or put child in between them.

Getting Along After Divorce

There is no question that after divorce you're going to have to set some rules to get along for the sake of the children, if nothing else. Getting along also helps you to live a less stress filled life after divorce. Here are some tips to put into practice so that you can make a divorce as easy as possible on the children.

Set up boundaries

You're going to have to set up some rules that both of you agree to follow. Do this from the beginning by deciding the things that you will and will not talk about. If you know that you have specific topics that cause conflict, decide that you will not discuss thatunless you're both calm. Focus on discussing the issues that relate to the kids and doing what is in the best interest of them.

Sometimes you will disagree

You're going to have to agree to disagree on some issues. Some of this will be worked out during the divorce using attorneys and the court system. However, raising kids is something that has to be handled between co-parents. Issues are going to come up with children, and parents have to be ready to create a united front and deal with them. Both people need to decide that anything that's done we'll be in the best interests of the children. Come up with a plan for what happens if there is a difference of opinion. Either there should be a time for cooling off or someone who can serve as a tiebreaker, such as a pastor or trusted family friend. Obviously, this last option should be used sparingly as two parents should be able to discuss calmly what is the best for their children.

Communication

If you have been in a volatile marriage, you might have become accustomed to not speaking or even slamming doors when you get mad. This won't work after a divorce. It's critical to continue communicating for the benefit of the children. Remember that your kids are watching how you communicate with each other, and it can taint their ability to communicate with their future spouse. Use your maturity and be the bigger person even if your ex-spouse is trying to incite an argument.

Be honest

No matter what caused the divorce, that needs to be put behind you. It can be very difficult if someone cheated on you because you want to continue being angry and not forgetting. However, for the sake of the kids you must build a bridge and set up rules that you won't talk about the past and the mistakes that happened. Instead, it all focus will be on the kids and how you can best raise them as co-parents.

Be willing to be back up

As hard as it might be if you're still angry at your ex-spouse, sometimes you need to back them up. If the child is trying to take advantage of the situation, it's important for you to stand your ground and back up the other parent if they're right. Set up rules that apply in both homes. That way, there is no question as to whether the child violated rules and require discipline.

Keep adult problems between the adults

Do not discuss the issues going on between you and your ex-spouse with your children. They should be allowed to remain kids and not be stressed out or exposed to adult problems. Keep them out of these issues as much as possible. Don't be critical and talk badly about your ex because your child will resent you for it later.

Don't sweat the small stuff

Your ex-spouse is going to get under your skin from time to time. If they remarry, their new spouse may aggravate you as well. Learn to let go of the small things so that you're not constantly in a state of conflict with them. Be willing to let some things go and only discuss the major issues that are deal breakers.

Make major decisions together

Vow to make all major decisions about your children together. These are decisions that could have a major impact on the rest of their life. For instance, if you are assisting them with the choice of college or career, or one of your children end up with a teenage pregnancy, these are major life decisions that both parents should be involved in.

Other situations that must be discussed are drug addiction, legal problems, hospitalization, putting the child on major medication or the child getting surgery. None of these should be things that one parent is surprised by or finds out about later. Each parent should be involved in making sure that the child is healthy and safe.

One of the most critical factors that you have to remember after a divorce is that you need to leave past hurts in the past. Don't allow things that happened within the marriage to cloud the way that you allow your child to have a relationship with your ex-spouse. Let those things stay in the past since they cannot be changed. Bringing them up only serves to keep you stuck in a place of negativity. That negativity will continue permeating the relationship that you have with your child, but also the relationship that you are trying to build as a co-parent with your ex-spouse.

Encourage the other parent to do the right thing when it comes to your children. Praise them when they do something right and show appreciation for their efforts. If you make a mistake, apologize. Wipe the slate clean because you're never going to be married to this person again. There's nothing that either one of you can do to go back and change the past. You have to move forward into the future by forgiving even if you don't forget.

Never criticize the other parent's relationship with their child. You want the child to feel love from all sides and have the security they need to be emotionally intelligent as adults. Never make them feel like the other parent doesn't love them. This will come back to haunt you as your criticisms will turn into them resenting you later.

In the end, if you can't work through this in the right way then you need to get help. See a therapist so that you can work through the hurt and anger that was left over from the divorce. If the child needs to go to counseling, go with them. This could happen months or even years after a divorce if things were not handled properly. Whatever it takes, do it for the long term emotional health of your child.

Divorce is never anyone's first choice. When we get married, we plan to be together for life. Unfortunately, for about half the couples in the U.S., there is no fairytale ending. Instead, they end up in divorce court after hiring expensive lawyers. Splitting up a home, especially one with kids, is difficult and disappointing when you had planned to be together always. Making the process and transition as easy as possible is important for the kids. Parents must learn to work together as parenting partners even though the marriage didn't make it. This will help to create emotionally intelligent kids who understand that life will sometimes hand you lemons, but you have to learn how to make lemonade. Even though things don't always work out, kids must learn that maturity is important and that treating everyone, including exes, with respect will lead to less stress and a happier life.

Chapter 23: Mapping Your Child's Adventure

When I was a 'tweener, the Scholastic Book Fair at our elementary school always had a nice selection of the, "Choose Your Own Adventure" series of books.The fun of these books is that each chapter ended with a choice, a choice that would drastically affect the outcome of the story.Make a good choice, and the adventure would continue.Make a bad choice and the story became stunted-short.In a way these stories, with their ever-changing tales, mirror life.

Life is an adventure unique to each and every one of us.Maybe no one told you that each chapter of your life ends with a choice that dramatically effects which direction your adventure goes.What is an adventure to one, is a prison to another.I have a friend who truly enjoys his accounting adventure.I would rather scoop the grease traps of fast food restaurants with my own, personal spoon.Both of us are right.Both of us are wrong.What is right for him, is wrong for me, and visa versa.We each have our own adventure and it would be wrong for me to make my friend feel any less of a person for the adventure that he finds most enjoyable.

No place is this truer than with our children.I must admit that until January of 2008, I had a tainted view of one, Earl Woods.So often we see offspring driven like Tiger Woods, and we are quick to assume that the parent has pushed his adventure on the child.Yet the Golf Digest story in that month's issue (January 2008) had a story from Tiger of his childhood that showed Earl Woods to be a man who saw a boy's adventure and helped his son map that adventure out.Earl proudly served our country.Because Tiger was too young to play on the Base Golf Course, he would 'sneak' on to the course in the late afternoon with his dad and play until light no longer permitted.According to Woods, the rule was that once darkness descended, if Tiger lost his golf ball, the game was over.Because of his desire to continue playing, Tiger learned quickly to know what his swing felt like and how that affected the flight of his ball.All of this so he could simply keep finding that dimpled sphere.

You see, all that ability we have seen in Tiger Woods is not by accident.True, Tiger has a natural affinity for the game of golf.However, his father recognized this at a young age and found ways to help Tiger 'map out' his own adventure.In this respect, Earl Woods set an example for us all.Recognizing his son's natural ability for the game, Earl encouraged his son to not forsake his God-given gift.

As parents- men especially- we all want a 'Tiger' for a son.Many men push their sons to achieve what they never accomplished.We justify this, thinking we are pushing them into something we perceive as a 'better adventure' for their own good.Yet too often this 'play' results in spiteful, unhappy children.Each of us is born with a purpose- a bent.When we celebrate that 'bent' in our children, they smile and praise us as parents.When we show indifference or negativity toward what our children feel naturally drawn to, they scowl and condemn us as parents.We have to come to the ultimate parenting realization: the realization that I would rather my child becomes a happy garbage collector, than becomes a depressed doctor.

I worked with a man at one point that took great pride in his custodial duties.He would finish stripping and waxing a floor and then stand back with a look in his eyes similar to that of a Major League Baseball Player who just hit the game winning homerun.To see this was to truly understand that, according to his bent, he had just hit the game winning homerun.Because of men like him, we have beautiful floors in places like malls that we simply take for granted.Yet his parents must have celebrated his 'bent,' and because of this, he can take pleasure in the unique ability, with which, he has been blessed.

It all comes down to learning to praise your child's purpose.When we, as parents do not, we not only rob our children, but the world around them as well.Each of us was put on this planet for a reason.No reason is better than another.Having a more lucrative job will not, necessarily, lead to a happier life.Your child might be happiest working for the Forest Service at a Fire Watch Tower.Yet if you steer your child improperly, she might end up in an ivory tower: 'better off' fiscally, but secretly miserable.

Every purpose has its own currency.Our codependent society pushes the ideal that everyone needs the 'toys' that everyone else desires.We celebrate rappers who seem to go from the projects to the penthouse.Yet we do not celebrate the child born in the penthouse, who finds ultimate fulfillment in teaching in the projects.Nor do we celebrate the doctor from the projects, who goes back to those neighborhoods to practice medicine, even though a more lucrative opportunity is readily available and waiting for her.

Yet the latter two examples are typically content- the real form of happiness.Hip-Hop stars rap endlessly about what they possess and all the girls they have 'had.'Reality is that when someone is trying to impress you with quantity, that person is typically anything but happy.Yet when you speak to those who constitute the latter two examples above, they will not speak of people they have used and abandoned, but rather of the people they have helped and propped up.When people truly enjoy their purpose, money is only ever an added bonus, not the real currency.

The last thing we need to grasp as parents when it comes to helping our children map out their adventure is that stereotypes interfere with the accuracy of the map.Our society has ignorantly tied 'bents' to sexuality, and this is tragically unfortunate.Occupational and sexual choices are separate crossroads that each person today must encounter.An artistic bent in a boy does not make him 'gay,' it makes him interesting and unique.

Each individual brings a unique approach to the overall 'bent,' with which, they are blessed.When we attach stereotypes to 'bents,' we either force a separate choice on a person, or we repulse them from their purpose.A boy, who chooses to love women and yet has an incredible, artistic bent, might choose a 'masculine' profession in order to assert his manhood to an ignorant parent.In doing this, the parent has inadvertently robbed the world of the next Van Gogh or Monnet.

Ultimately, we need to be students of our children.When we take the time with them, surround ourselves with people who make a positive impact on them and speak to our children in ways that celebrate who they are, we help them map their adventure.This being said, in as much as I would like to say that if you do these things, you will always have incredible, happy children, we have to accept that even if we do everything right, our children are individuals who ultimately make their own choices.

Chapter 24: How To Keep Emotionally Strong

No matter how well you internalize the importance of protecting your children and providing a healthy environment, you won't be able to do it if you're falling apart. Protecting your own mental health is the first step in protecting your child's well-being. Remember that your children can't be your sole source of meaning. Find outside hobbies such as dancing, a sport, a volunteer group, or a book club, and regularly take time to do the things you love.

Don't be afraid to spend time away from your children. Even the best parents occasionally need a break, so work on developing a network of excellent caregivers who can watch your kids when you need help. If no one is available, put yourself in a time-out. Take a nap or take time to meditate if you feel like you're losing your cool; don't let your child see you throw a tantrum, or he'll learn that it's acceptable for him to do the same. Always demonstrate the behavior you expect from your child.

Professional help can play a significant role in helping you keep it together. Many adults seek therapy after a divorce, and there's no shame in doing so. If you're having trouble managing your emotions, a few appointments with a professional can help you gain the skills you need. Anti-depressants and anti-anxiety medications can also provide a temporary relief from the worst pain of divorce. Some other things you can do to keep your cool include:

Getting plenty of rest. Aim for seven to nine hours of sleep every night.

Venting to a friend or loved one – but doing so out of earshot of your child.

Spending a day at the spa, a sporting event, or with friends.

Taking a vacation when you need to – even if it's just a weekend getaway.

Eating a healthy diet. Starving yourself, overeating, or relying on fast food and takeout aren't healthy coping mechanisms, and a parent has a duty to model healthy eating habits to his or her child.

Steering clear of drugs, alcohol, and smoking. If you end up abusing a substance, don't let your child see it happen, and get help immediately. Many people find that they struggle with addiction after a divorce, and a therapist, a 12-step program, and or a doctor can help you move past the struggles of addiction.

Spending time with pets. Several studies have shown that the simple act of petting a dog or cat can help calm your nerves. Rather than getting frustrated by the endless demands of kids and a pet, try walking or training the dog together. You may find you end up feeling much calmer.

Chapter 25: Inevitable Leadership Skills That You Can Instill In Your Child.

A leader - a person who is followed willingly by a group of people, or even whole organizations; a person who leads a crowd. Why is the skill of leadership useful? Because it helps run a business, and make dreams come true. Every entrepreneur has a group of co-workers, because it's hard to run a company alone. A group working on the same task is more likely to get better results in a faster way.

Leadership is a combination of personal traits that allow people to take control over their own actions. It also allows to manage other people's responsibilities associated with a particular task. Some children are born with natural leadership traits and predispositions, and some aren't. Fortunately, a child can develop these traits by environment and upbringing. And that's what we'll discuss in this chapter.

Communication.

A leader may have extensive knowledge, and be able to do many things, but without any communication skills a leader will be much less effective (or not effective at all). That's why people should learn communication skills at an early age. The era of cell phones and computers is unfavorable, because it makes communication skills decline, even in adults. And when you need to make a business presentation, conduct negotiations, hire and fire employees, give praise or a reprimand, your body language or words may either help or do harm, when you're not aware how to use them.
So how do you teach your child to communicate?
- The example comes from the top.
Firstly, you teach your child by giving example. Show your child how to be both well-mannered and assertive in contacts with others. It's really important to

practice keeping eye contact when people are talk face to face. Explain the importance of eye contact to your child, and tell them that by keeping eye contact many things may still remain unspoken.

- Phone calls.

When you're talking on the phone in front of your child, make it a lesson out of it. You can even ask your child: "I'm having an important phone call now about this and that. What do you think I should say?" And then make the phone call in front of your child. When you talk on the phone, try to speak slow and clear.

- E-mails.

We use e-mail almost every day, but I bet not every adult can do it. When typing, we can't use facial expressions or gestures, or change our tone of voice, for example, to emphasize irony. We can only type words that may be interpreted in different ways. Therefore, an e-mail conversation with your child may be an interesting way of learning how to communicate. Take into account colloquial words, spelling, complimentary phrases, salutation and leave-taking. Of course, grammar is also very important. Your child will enjoy the opportunity of e-mail birthday-planning with you. And at the same time they will develop good e-mail habits.

Leading a team.

It's said that opportunity makes the thief. I'd say that opportunity makes the leader. Don't rely on school, as it'll teach your child how to obey general rules without questioning them. Create situations where your child can practice team-work and making decisions on behalf of the team. How?

You can do it while playing board games with the whole family. Ask your child (who is familiar with a chosen game) to explain the rules, answer potential questions, suggest the choice of pawns or position of the board, choose where you're going to play (on the floor, or a kitchen table).

On your child's birthday, ask your child to make a toast for all guests. Your child may also invite the guests to help themselves to the cake (you can practice such actions with your child a few days before the actual event, so that your child will be more confident. But I can guarantee that your child will volunteer to practice by the third time). P.S. This is a great opportunity for your child to learn how to communicate and speak publicly. Have you noticed that it's a nightmare for some adults?

Creativity.

Every entrepreneur should be creative. If your child comes up with common ideas, it will make their company common too, and we don't want that to happen.General creativity may be practiced in different ways. And you also, dear parent, may be creative! First, don't limit your child's natural creativity that is displayed in the process of exploring the world. Second, you can introduce some games to your child's everyday activities.

- On a warm, sunny day, lie on the grass and watch the clouds - it's a classic. You can guess with your child the shape of clouds. You turn on your stomachs and observe the ants. Then yyou try to guess what each of them could be thinking, and what they will do when they reach their destination. Can you be more creative? Of course! Try to think what an ant would be if it weren't an ant.

- During everyday household activities, chooseone item with your child, for example, a spoon. Then, try to come up with various ways of how to use the spoon. First five are a piece of cake. Another five are also easy. But after you reach ten examples, you have to think harder. When your brains come up with any possible ideas, the real creativity training begins.

There's also another side of creativity, that you can practice with older children, namely, marketing. It's not only an essential part of promoting a company, but also of promoting yourself. How to practice marketing?

Begin with observation. Look at billboards, leaflets, TV, radio and magazine ads - there are plenty of them, so you'll find your observation material easily. Every time discuss with your child an ad you see, for example, what draws their attention to this particular ad. Ask your child what they can call a marketing exercise in the ad (first, try to explain this difficult term in your own words). Together identify slogans, headlines, catch-phrases, so that your child knows the truth about ads. This knowledge will not only help them run their future business, but also make them more resistant to pervasive consumerism.

Then you can use your knowledge in practice. Are you organizing your child's birthday? Ask your child to make invitation cards.

If you're brave and eager: choose one item worth less than $20 from your house. Ask your child to make up an eBay offer, so the item sells for $50. It's similar to doing homework, but children love this method in practice. You can ask your child to analyze other eBay offers, and list marketing exercises, such as: free shipping, bonuses, 2 in 1, choice of packaging or color, personal receipt.

To summarize: As you know, the term leader isn't defined in a clear way, because there are many types of leaders (which will be discussed in the next chapter). But all of these types need the traits I've discussed in this chapter. And you may start practicing these traits with your child today. Good luck!

Chapter 26: Emotions And Communication

The Distance

There will be gaps between your child's understanding of the world and your own. In some cases, children literally do not yet have the mental resources to comply with your wishes. For instance, children younger than three often cannot focus on tasks for much longer than a few minutes, and will not be able to improve their focus until their attention spans finish developing. It can be difficult to understand the speech patterns of children younger than three, and they may have just as difficult a time understanding yours.

Most importantly, children generally do not have the verbal skills you do, and in some cases, misunderstandings between parents and children are based on simple problems with translating between each other's speech patterns. A well-known experiment in child psychology involved presenting young children with a picture of four red roses and two white roses. They children were asked: 'are there more red flowers or flowers?' The idea is to test whether or not they understood that the red and white flowers were both part of the same set. Many children answered 'more red flowers.'

However, this experiment has been repeated decades later, showing vastly different results. When the wording of the question was changed to more specific language, a significantly larger portion of the children in the study got the question right. The kids tested in the original experiment may have just assumed that the experimenter was asking them to compare the number of red and white flowers. These kids may well have been surprised years later, when they found out what happened with the test results and how it affected public opinion about what children know. Anyone with vivid memories of their own childhood could probably relate similar events like this: having certain thoughts you want to articulate, but lacking the verbal skills to do so, understanding why the adults around you are failing to understand you, but lacking the ability to make this clear to them.

Parents should keep that in mind when getting into casual disagreements with their children. One of the greatest virtues in any parent is patience. Children do not have the emotional control or the powers of expression of adults, especially when they are very young. Parents are there to help instill in them the tools to respect and acknowledge the feelings, needs, and wants of others. If parents can keep their cool and learn how to help their kids through those earlier periods, they will be rewarded with well-behaved children when their kids are older.

Parents should try to avoid taking certain things their children do or say too seriously. Kids can say mean things that they do not even understand, let alone intend to be hurtful. Often times, they may just be trying to get a reaction out of you, and you are better off not encouraging them. Essentially, parents need to compartmentalize their feelings as best as they can when dealing with children. It is much easier said than done, but kids learning to respect others needs and boundaries is part of their development. It will not last forever.

Managing anger can be challenging for some people. Some parents may be concerned about the nurturing parent model, and wonder whether they can remain as patient as necessary for inductive discipline to work properly. People with ongoing anger management problems should seek treatment, preferably before they start raising children. However, almost everyone gets frustrated at some point as parents. As with all situations involving strong anger, it helps to take a step back and ask yourself about the situation. What can you do, what is going on, and what are other ways to frame the situation? Is your child trying to communicate something else? What can you do to make the situation better? Parents who are overwhelmed by anger should leave the wrong and remove themselves from the situation.

Thinking rationally about the situation will be better for both of you. Things can be said in the heat of the moment that parents can regret bitterly, but they cannot take them back, and children are sensitive to almost everything that happens to them in their early years.

Praise and Encouragement

Doting parents may praise their children almost unknowingly, out of pure affection. Giving almost instantaneous praise to young children for most things they do is actually very useful. Babies and toddlers respond well to the positive emotions of those around them, and being praised for even the simplest things is just the sort of positive reinforcement they need to go about exploring the world. As children get older, it is important for parents to temper and monitor the types and quantities of praise they give their children. One of the best ways to praise children to focus on how much effort they put into tasks, whatever those asks are, especially as they get older.

As children get older, they get much better at distinguishing naked praise from informed praise. Complimenting everything they do, regardless of how much or how little effort they put into it, is useful for young children. As children get older, they will become immune to almost all praise if the adults around it give it with almost no discernible provocation. It is tempting, especially for parents with potentially gifted children, to praise children based on their abilities.

Unfortunately, this sort of praise often hurts children's self-confidence rather than building it.

Children begin to internalize the idea that skills are something you just have, rather than something you develop and nurture. As such, they make take their struggles with the mastery of certain tasks as evidence that they do not actually have those skills. They may avoid certain challenges instead of taking on new challenges as opportunities for growth. Everyone, no matter how intelligent, will still face challenges as they learn, and that works doubly so for children whose brains are still rapidly developing.

Praising children based on the effort they put into tasks encourages them to challenge themselves and prove their abilities, rather than using those abilities as a sort of security blanket. Praising children for the completion of a long and unpleasant task may be valuable. Less so, however, is praising them for something they may like doing anyway. A child who likes to read and who gets unduly praised for doing so may question his or her own motivations for why he or she likes to read, and get less pleasure out of reading as a result. In situations like these, it may be better to try to engage with your children. Asking them about what books they are reading, and talking to them about how much you enjoy reading, can make it a fun mutual activity. Letting kids appreciate just how much fun certain things are will give them whole new ways of motivating themselves in the future.

Conclusion

It's clear to see that those children who fare the best through the process of divorce are those who have two parents who are prepared to put their differences and disagreements aside in order to continue being the best parents they can be.

No one is saying that the process itself is easy, but with continued work and some give and take between the two parents you can enjoy a better relationship with their children and make the process of them growing up as smooth as possible.

No matter how much you may try to work against it, divorce is a fact of life and it can and does happen to couples for various reasons every single day. When there are children involved the processes that the couple must go through need to bear them in mind before anything else.

It is in everyone's best interests to remain civil and polite during every stage of the divorce process, and taking a step back before you consider your response to any given situation quite often results in a better outcome for all concerned.

And especially for the children.

www.ingramcontent.com/pod-product-compliance
Lightning Source LLC
Chambersburg PA
CBHW072011070526
44583CB00015B/1438